FOR WHOM THE BELL TOLLS

Ernest Hemingway's Undiscovered Country

TWAYNE'S MASTERWORK STUDIES

Robert Lecker, General Editor

FOR WHOM THE BELL TOLLS

Ernest Hemingway's Undiscovered Country

Allen Josephs

TWAYNE PUBLISHERS • NEW YORK
Maxwell Macmillan Canada • *Toronto*
Maxwell Macmillan International • *New York Oxford Singapore Sydney*

Twayne's Masterwork Studies No. 138

For Whom the Bell Tolls: Ernest Hemingway's Undiscovered Country
Allen Josephs

Twayne Publishers   Maxwell Macmillan Canada, Inc.
Macmillan Publishing Company   1200 Eglinton Avenue East
866 Third Avenue   Suite 200
New York, New York 10022   Don Mills, Ontario M3C 3N1

Library of Congress Cataloging-in-Publication Data

Josephs, Allen.
    For whom the bell tolls : Ernest Hemingway's undiscovered country / by Allen
Josephs.
        p.   cm.—(Twayne's masterwork studies ; no. 138)
    Includes bibliographical references and index.
    ISBN 0-8057-8078-5—ISBN 0-8057-4456-8 (pbk.)
    1. Hemingway, Ernest, 1899–1961. For whom the bell tolls. 2. Spain—History—
Civil War, 1936–1939—Literature and the war. I. Title. II. Series.
PS3515.E37F6   1994   94-4017
813'.52—dc20   CIP

The paper used in this publication meets the minimum requirements of American
National Standard for Information Sciences—Permanence of Paper for Printed Library
Materials. ANSI Z3948-1984. ∞ ™

10 9 8 7 6 5 4 3 2 1 (hc)
10 9 8 7 6 5 4 3 2 1 (pb)

Printed in the United States of America

This book is for my father,
Josef Ernest Josephs,
who taught me the worth of words
and the flight of Pegasus.

Contents

Illustrations

Hemingway at the front lines during the battle of Teruel, around 21 December 1937. Photographer Robert Capa caught Hemingway helping a Republican soldier unjam his rifle.

Robert Capa/Magnum Photos. Courtesy of the Hemingway Collection, John F. Kennedy Library. (Photo no. EH 4736P)

Note on the References and Acknowledgments

The first edition of *For Whom the Bell Tolls* was published in 1940 by Charles Scribner's Sons. All subsequent editions are based on that text, so I have used it for parenthetical page references. The text itself has errors, mostly in Spanish (see Appendix: On Language), but it remains the only "standard" text until such time as the publishers decide a corrected one would be worthwhile. I have kept the published text in my citations, and I have kept Hemingway's correspondence as he wrote it. In order not to be confusing, I have also kept the Spanish names as Hemingway used them (e.g., Rafael el Gallo instead of Rafael *el gallo*, as it should be in Spanish). I have corrected the accents in names when I refer to the characters in other than direct citations (i.e., where Hemingway writes Maria or Gonzalez, I have used María and González).

Many people helped me with this book, some of whom are acknowledged in the text, footnotes, and bibliography. Others, however, deserve mention here. Thanks first of all to my Hemingway students over the years—the toughest and best critics of all—with special mention to Cheryl Carlos, Tracy Cox, Becky Fulcher, Gerald Kniendl, Bob Patroni, Sonja Thames, and April Woodham, all of whom influenced my thinking about *For Whom the Bell Tolls*.

I am also grateful to many friends and colleagues who went to extra lengths to help me: Susan Beegel, Sandy Forman, Robin Gajdusek, Don Junkins, Bernice Kert, Bob Lewis, Bob Martin, Tod Oliver, Mike

Reynolds, Wolfie Rudat, Paul Smith, H. R. Stoneback, Will Watson (who kept my Spanish politics straight), the late Jim Hinkle, and many other members of the Hemingway Society. Also thanks to the late Juan Benet, Juan Caballero, Tomás Entwhistle, Martha Gellhorn, Greg Lanier, Phil Momberger, Don Pohren, C. P. Scanlon, and Michael Wigram. At the John F. Kennedy Library, thanks to Megan Desnoyers, Allan Goodrich, Lisa Middents, and Joan O'Connor. At ICONA, thanks to Gregorio Cobos, Javier Donés Pastor, and Venancio González. Special thanks to Ed Stanton for relinquishing to me his erstwhile intended title, "The Undiscovered Country." And last, but far from least, thanks to Kay Martin for her loyal and accurate manuscript management and indexing.

Inevitably some of the ideas in this study come from my previous work. The following articles have in some measure contributed to what I have said here: "Hemingway and the Spanish Civil War, or the Volatile Mixture of Politics and Art," in Brown et al., eds., *Rewriting the Good Fight: Critical Essays on the Literature of the Spanish Civil War* (East Lansing: Michigan State University Press, 1989); "Hemingway's Spanish Civil War Stories, or the Spanish Civil War as Reality," in Susan F. Beegel, ed., *Hemingway's Neglected Short Fiction: New Perspectives* (Ann Arbor: UMI Research Press, 1989; reprinted by University of Alabama Press, 1992); "In Another Country: Hemingway and Spain," *North Dakota Quarterly* 60 (Spring 1992, Special issue: *Malraux, Hemingway and Embattled Spain*): 50–57; "Reality and Invention in *For Whom the Bell Tolls*, or Reflections on the Nature of the Historical Novel" in Ken Rosen, ed., *Hemingway Repossessed* (Westport, Conn: Praeger, 1994); and "Love in *For Whom the Bell Tolls*" in Joseph Waldmeir and Frederick Joseph Svoboda, eds., *Hemingway in Michigan and the World* (East Lansing: Michigan State University Press, 1994).

Chronology: Ernest Hemingway's Life and Works

1899   Ernest Miller Hemingway born 21 July in fashionable Chicago suburb of Oak Park, Illinois, first son, second child of Dr. Clarence Edmonds Hemingway and Grace Hall Hemingway. Father, physician and naturalist, teaches Ernest hunting, fishing, love of nature. Mother, singer and voice teacher, teaches him music, creativity. Strict Congregationalist upbringing and public school education: sports, especially fishing and hunting, school newspaper, and literary magazine. Spends summers at family cottage on Lake Walloon in northern Michigan.

1917   Graduates Oak Park High School. In October begins writing job as reporter for *Kansas City Star*.

1918   Joins American Red Cross ambulance unit bound for Italy. Night of 8 July severely wounded by shrapnel from Austrian mortar and machine-gun fire at Fossalta; nevertheless, carries a man to safety. Later awarded Italy's Croce al Merito di Guerra. Recuperates in Milan. Falls in love with nurse, Agnes Von Kurowsky.

1919   Returns home, stopping briefly in Gibraltar and southern Spain. Begins writing stories. Receives "Dear John" letter from Agnes. Fishes in Michigan where he spends summer and fall.

1920   Writes for *Toronto Star*. Summers at Lake Walloon. Moves to Chicago in October after fight with mother. Begins magazine editing. Meets Sherwood Anderson, other Chicago writers. Also meets Hadley Richardson of St. Louis.

1921   Edits *Cooperative Commonwealth*. Marries Hadley in September. Sails with her to France in December, stopping briefly at Vigo in northern Spain.

1922   As correspondent for *Toronto Star*, travels much of Europe. Becomes part of Paris literary scene, meeting James Joyce, Gertrude Stein, Ezra Pound, and others. Hadley loses all his manuscripts in December.

1923   Skis in Switzerland; visits Pound in Rapallo, Italy. Makes first extended trip to Spain in May and June. Sees *corridas* (bullfights) in Madrid and provinces. In July returns to Spain for fiesta of San Fermín in Pamplona. Publishes *Three Stories and Ten Poems*. Returns with Hadley to Toronto for birth of John Hadley Nicanor Hemingway. Quits *Toronto Star*.

1924   Returns to Paris with writing as sole career. Writes eight of best stories in three months. Edits for Ford Madox Ford's *transatlantic review*. Publishes *in our time* in Paris. Spends June and July in Spain seeing corridas.

1925   Boni and Liveright publishes *In Our Time*, expanded version. Attends San Fermín festival with Paris friends. Writes rough draft of *The Sun Also Rises*, based loosely on that experience. Writes *Torrents of Spring*. Winters in Schruns, Austria, rewriting, fictionalizing *The Sun Also Rises*.

1926   Boni and Liveright rejects *Torrents of Spring*. Hemingway signs with Scribner's, his publisher for life. Spends part of May, July, August, October in Spain. Ernest and Hadley separate in August. Scribner's publishes *The Sun Also Rises* in October.

1927   Marries Pauline Pfeiffer in May, becoming formally Catholic. Spends July, August, September in Spain. Publishes *Men Without Women* in October.

1928   Leaves Europe for Key West, Florida, via Havana, stopping at Vigo and Canary Islands (Spain). Works on *A Farewell to Arms*. Second son, Patrick, born in Kansas City, Mo. Hunts in Wyoming in summer. On 6 December, Ernest's father commits suicide with .32 Smith and Wesson revolver.

1929   Returns to Paris with Pauline via Spanish ports, then returns to Spain for July and August for *corridas*, fishing. In September meets and admires American matador Sidney Franklin. *A Farewell to Arms* published in September. In October stock market begins to fall, and world depression follows.

1930   Establishes residence in Key West. Works on *Death in the Afternoon*. Hunts, fishes, works in Wyoming and Montana. Sells movie rights to *A Farewell to Arms*. Suffers severe fracture of right arm in auto accident.

Chronology

1931   Broken arm prevents work in spring. Spends May to mid-September in Spain following corridas and working on *Death in the Afternoon*. Third son Gregory Hancock born in Kansas City in November.

1932   Finishes *Death in the Afternoon* in January. Works on new stories. Fishes for marlin in Cuba. Summers in Wyoming. *Death in the Afternoon* published to mixed reviews in September.

1933   Pioneers marlin fishing in Cuba in spring and early summer. Signs on to write for new men's magazine, *Esquire*. Goes to Spain for corridas late summer, early fall. *Winner Take Nothing* published to mixed reviews in October. Safari in East Africa at year's end.

1934   Continues safari in spite of dysentery. Fishes Indian Ocean. Returns to Key West and buys fishing boat, the *Pilar*. Fishes, works on African materials, writes pieces for *Esquire*.

1935   Spends spring and summer fishing at Bimini. Writes *Esquire* pieces. After devastating Labor Day hurricane, writes piece for *New Masses* blaming Washington bureaucrats for many deaths. *Green Hills of Africa* published in October to mixed reviews.

1936   Fishes at Bimini. Publishes "The Snows of Kilimanjaro" in *Esquire* and "The Short Happy Life of Francis Macomber" in *Cosmopolitan*. On 18 July Spanish Civil War begins. Hunts and fishes in Wyoming. Works on Harry Morgan stories. Contributes money for ambulances for Spanish Republic. Agrees to cover Spanish Civil War for the North American Newspaper Alliance (NANA). In December meets Martha Gellhorn at Sloppy Joe's in Key West.

1937   Writes part of narration for pro-Republican film, *Spain in Flames*. Spends mid-March to mid-May in Spain. Helps with Joris Ivens's film *The Spanish Earth* at Jarama front. Visits battle sites near Guadalajara where Republicans defeated troops sent by Mussolini to aid Franco. Ernest and Martha observe running battle of Madrid. Their hotel, the Florida, is shelled frequently. Spends ten days in Guadarrama mountains, touring zone on horseback with Martha. Addresses Writers' Congress in New York in June. Writes narration for *The Spanish Earth* and shows film with Ivens at White House and in Hollywood. Returns to Spain in fall to cover war. *To Have and Have Not* published to mixed reviews in October. Possibly takes part in guerrilla operation north of Teruel. Writes his only play, *The Fifth Column*.

1938   Writes for *Ken* magazine on Spanish Civil War. Spends April and May in Spain, reporting on Ebro front. Summers in Key West. Returns to Paris in fall to work on Spanish Civil War stories. *The Fifth Column and the First Forty-Nine Stories* published to mixed reviews in October. Returns briefly to Spanish Civil War for fourth and last time in November.

1939   In March in Cuba begins work on *For Whom the Bell Tolls*. Spanish Civil War over 1 April. Rents Finca Vigía with Martha. Arrives Wyoming late summer as war breaks out in Europe. Breaks with Pauline. Goes to Sun Valley, Idaho, with Martha. Continues work on *For Whom the Bell Tolls*.

1940   Writes *For Whom the Bell Tolls* all spring. Finishes before forty-first birthday in July. Goes to Sun Valley in September. *For Whom the Bell Tolls* published 21 October. Most reviews, except from political left, are very positive. *For Whom the Bell Tolls* becomes Book of the Month selection; sells to Paramount for record price. In November, Pauline's divorce final, and Ernest marries Martha in Cheyenne, Wyoming. Buys Finca Vigía in December.

1941   Accompanies Martha to China and Far East. Although *For Whom the Bell Tolls* is unanimous choice for Pulitzer Prize, veto by chairman of the board (president of Columbia University) blocks award. Spends summer in Cuba, fall in Sun Valley. *For Whom the Bell Tolls* sells over half a million copies, wins Limited Editions Club Gold Medal. Is driving home through Texas when Pearl Harbor is bombed.

1942   Organizes short-lived counterintelligence operation in Cuba, nicknamed "Crook Factory," to ferret out Nazi spies, sympathizers. Sets up *Pilar* as antisubmarine patrol boat. Edits and writes introduction for *Men at War* anthology.

1943   Continues to operate *Pilar*. Film of *For Whom the Bell Tolls* premieres 10 July. Ernest hopes never to see it. Martha leaves for Europe in October. *For Whom the Bell Tolls* reaches 785,000 copies in U.S.; 100,000 in England. Writes nothing for the year.

1944   Goes to England in May as war correspondent for *Collier's*. Meets Mary Welsh. Suffers severe concussion in auto accident. From July on, covers war on continent, attaching himself to U.S. Fourth Infantry. Continues liaison with Mary.

1945   Returns to Cuba to prepare Finca for Mary's arrival. Mary divorces her husband and Martha divorces Ernest.

Chronology

Begins work on *The Garden of Eden*. Marries Mary in March. Saves her life in August when ectopic pregnancy causes fallopian tube to rupture. Spends late summer and fall in Sun Valley.

1947   Works on *Garden of Eden* in Cuba. Receives Bronze Star for meritorious service as war correspondent. Spends fall in Sun Valley.

1948   Spends spring and summer in Cuba. Returns to Italy in fall. Meets Adriana Ivancich.

1949   Begins work on *Across the River and into the Trees* in Italy. Returns to Cuba in spring. Works on novel in summer and fall, modeling Renata on nineteen-year-old Adriana. Finishes in Paris before Christmas.

1950   Winters in Italy. Returns to Cuba in April. *Across the River and into the Trees* published in September to negative reviews, but sells well. Works on *Islands in the Stream*.

1951   Writes *The Old Man and the Sea* in January and February. Works on *Islands in the Stream*. His mother dies in June, Pauline in October.

1952   Fulgencio Batista takes power in Cuba with military coup. Ernest works on new material, "The Last Good Country," about Michigan in his youth. *Life* publishes *The Old Man and the Sea* on 1 September, Scribner's on 8 September, to rave reviews, extraordinary sales. Cuban government awards him Medal of Honor.

1953   Wins Pulitzer Prize in May. Returns to Spain for first time in fifteen years, seeing corridas in Pamplona, Madrid, Valencia. Begins extended safari in East Africa.

1954   Continues African stay. Severely injured in second of two plane crashes in two days. Recuperates in Italy, then goes to Spain for corridas, but never fully recovers. Home in Cuba in July. Wins Nobel Prize in October. Liver and kidney infections at year's end.

1955   Remains in Cuba working on unpublished "African book." Fishes and recuperates. Works on fishing sequences for film of *The Old Man and the Sea* in Cuba.

1956   Goes to Peru to catch marlin for film of *The Old Man and the Sea*. Spends fall in Spain going to corridas. Finishes year in Paris.

1957   Returns to Cuba, ill and depressed. In fall begins *A Moveable Feast*.

1958   Works on *A Moveable Feast* through July. Works on rewrites of *The Garden of Eden*. Goes west for fall, renting house in Ketchum, Idaho.

1959   Batista falls; Fidel Castro takes over Cuba in January. Ernest buys house in Ketchum, returns home briefly to Cuba, and goes to Spain. Sees season of corridas, from May through October, especially rivalry between Antonio Ordóñez and Luis Miguel Dominguín. Works on *The Dangerous Summer*, finishing the year at Ketchum.

1960   Works on *The Dangerous Summer* in Cuba. Returns to Spain in August. Suffers severe depression. *Life* publishes parts of *The Dangerous Summer* in September. Hospitalized at Mayo Clinic in November for electroshock treatment.

1961   At Mayo Clinic in January continues to suffer severe depression and illness, including high blood pressure, liver and kidney disease, diabetes, possibly hemochromatosis. In Ketchum works on *A Moveable Feast*, seems to recover slightly. Depression returns. Readmitted to Mayo Clinic late April to end of June. On 2 July, in Ketchum commits suicide with shotgun. Buried 5 July in Ketchum cemetery.

Introduction

Until he ran across the passage from John Donne in the *Oxford Book of English Prose* that gave him the definitive title for his novel, Hemingway's favorite—of some twenty-six titles he had been thinking about—was *The Undiscovered Country*.[1] *For Whom the Bell Tolls* may be a more poetic title, but *The Undiscovered Country* is a more accurate description of what Hemingway was really about in this novel of the Spanish Civil War. The phrase comes from act 3, scene 1 of *Hamlet* and refers there to death: "The undiscovered country from whose bourn / No traveller returns. . . . " But in the novel it encompasses much more than death. The "undiscovered country" suggests, particularly in Hemingway's view, the nature of Spain itself; more specifically, within the novel it hints at the unknown but fateful and omen-ridden nature of the episode of blowing the bridge; for Robert Jordan and María it also describes the ecstasy of love and, finally, for Robert Jordan, the ultimate uncertainty of death. I chose to use the phrase in the title of this book because, above all, the "undiscovered country" is the realm of the artist's imagination where all the other elements are given a life of their own.

LITERARY AND HISTORICAL CONTEXT

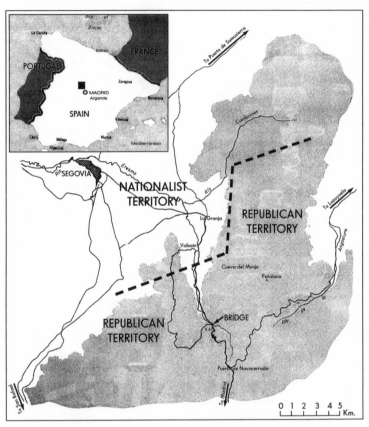

The heavy broken line shows the approximate location of the real front. The actual battle took place slightly to the north of that line as the Republican (Loyalist) troops advanced. The shaded area represents altitudes higher than 1200 meters. Notice that the location of the bridge is not behind the lines but well within Republican territory. Hemingway's placed the bridge behind the lines (i.e., within Nationalist territory) to suit his fictional purposes.

Map by Sandra Forman and Paul Goodwin (after J. M. Martínez Bande).

1

Historical Context: The Writer's Problem

Ernest Hemingway was nervous and hot on the sultry New York evening of 4 June 1937, as he prepared to make one of the few public speeches of his life. Addressing an audience of 3,500 at the Writers' Congress, sponsored by the League of American Authors at Carnegie Hall, he began by saying: "A writer's problem does not change. He himself changes, but his problem remains the same. It is always how to write truly and having found what is true, to project it in such a way that it becomes part of the experience of the person who reads it." That simple declaration came as close as anything Hemingway ever expressed to defining his own artistic ambition, and it described precisely the problem he would face two years later when he began his longest and most ambitious novel, *For Whom the Bell Tolls*.

As Hemingway continued his speech that night, he remarked that really good writers were rewarded by "any existing system of government that they can tolerate," and that there was "only one form of government that cannot produce good writers, and that system is fascism. For fascism is a lie told by bullies. A writer who will not lie cannot live and work under fascism." His speech took the hall—and its largely leftist audience—by storm. Recently returned from the year-old

3

Spanish Civil War where he was serving as a war correspondent for the North American Newspaper Alliance (NANA), Ernest Hemingway had now publicly and unequivocally joined the fight against fascism. As one witness remarked, "How could this fight be lost now, with Hemingway on our side?" (Baker 1969, 314) This committed and sustained antifascism would become another determining factor in the writing of *For Whom the Bell Tolls*.

Hemingway had not always been so committed. His first novel, *The Sun Also Rises*, dealt with the traumas, both physical and psychological, of the aftermath of World War I. His second major novel, *A Farewell to Arms*, portrayed a disaffected soldier who makes his own separate peace. During the 1930s, in the wake of worldwide economic collapse, many American writers made a marked swing to the political Left, and a number of them embraced communism as a solution to social and economic woes.

But Hemingway was neither a leftist nor a joiner. During the early thirties he lived and fished down in Key West, Florida, went to *corridas* in Spain, and made an extended safari to Africa. *Death in the Afternoon*, his treatise on Spain and the bulls published in 1932, and *Green Hills of Africa*, his account of the safari published in 1935, along with stories such as "The Snows of Kilimanjaro" published in *Esquire* in 1936, and "The Short Happy Life of Francis Macomber" published in *Cosmopolitan* the same year, began to earn him a reputation as a celebrity and sportsman. But in many literary circles he was considered a callous anti-intellectual, impervious to social concerns.

When civil war erupted in Spain in July 1936, Hemingway was naturally concerned because he loved Spain and had many friends there on both sides and because he understood the overarching political implications of the conflict. Although always inclined toward the Republic, his only immediate commitment to that side was to raise money for ambulances.

On 5 February 1937 he wrote somewhat dispassionately to Catholic writer Harry Sylvester, "The Spanish war is a bad war, Harry, and nobody is right." Four days later he started a letter to his wife's family, "This is from the leader of the Ingrates Battalion on the wrong side of the Spanish war." The wrong side? Hemingway was lamely joking because he thought the Pfeiffer family, being Catholic, would not support the Republic.

In a more serious vein he continued, "The Reds may be as bad as they say but they are the people of the country versus the absentee landlords, the moors, the italians and the Germans" (I have kept EH's eccentricities in his correspondence throughout). He finished by predicting, "This is the dress rehearsal for the inevitable European war and I would like to try to write anti-war war correspondence that would help to keep us out of it when it comes."[1]

There are a number of notable comments in this letter, but to start with, there are Hemingway's vaguely neutralist and isolationist statements, probably meant to appease his Catholic in-laws, that he could be an "anti-war" war correspondent and that he could help "us" stay "out of it." Both those notions, however lightly he meant them at the time, had changed radically by June when, after two months at the fronts in Spain, he addressed fellow writers at Carnegie Hall. In February Hemingway could still sound like his old reluctant anti-war novelist self, although there is good reason, such as monetary contributions, to believe he was already committed to the Republic. In any case by June he was speaking publicly for the only political cause he ever really espoused.

On the other hand, Hemingway was certain from early on about the Spanish Civil War being the dress rehearsal for "the inevitable European war." He had been an astute observer of European politics since the early twenties when he served as European correspondent for the *Toronto Star*, and his political acumen stood him in good stead in this prediction.

Finally there is the matter of the "Reds . . . the moors, the italians and the Germans." All readers of *For Whom the Bell Tolls* at some point have to face the complex issues of the Spanish Civil War because that war is the immediate context of *For Whom the Bell Tolls*. Even though Hemingway would remove much of the novel's action from the events of the real war, the novel finally cannot be understood without understanding the nature of the actual conflict. And what is even more crucial, the issues in Spain, as Hemingway fully understood from the beginning, were the issues of a much larger European and worldwide struggle between the Right and the Left.

To state it as simply as possible, the Spanish Civil War began as the result of a partially foiled right-wing coup attempt by the army (Nationalists) against the democratically elected, leftist-led, Spanish Republic (Loyalists). Although cities in the south fell to General Francisco Franco's airlifted forces invading from Africa, and cities in the north to General Emilio Mola's army forces, Madrid and other major cities did not fall, and the populace armed itself to stop the army's march on the capital. That process turned the incomplete coup into a civil war, and the resulting people's militia is what Hemingway meant in his letter by "the people of the country." Many of Franco's initial invading troops were regular Moroccan soldiers and that is what he meant by "moors."

The Spanish combatants themselves were comprised of legionaries, rebel army troops, and some of the civil guardsmen pitted against the hastily formed and politically splintered Loyalist militia (including a minority of still-loyal army forces). But from the beginning there was massive foreign intervention. Before July 1936 was out, Hitler had agreed to help Franco, and Mussolini had already begun sending him planes. A farcical nonintervention pact was signed by the European powers that allowed the democracies to keep from supporting the Republic. Germany and Italy signed the pact and then completely ignored it, using Spain as a testing ground for new military tactics, including the deliberate bombing of the civilian population. Aside from the inadequate International Brigades of volunteers, only the Soviets helped the Republic. These are what Hemingway called in his letter "the italians and the Germans" and the "Reds" respectively.

Politically the Germans and the Italians were fascists, of course, and the Soviets were communists, as were many of the volunteers in the International Brigades. It was in part their confrontation in Spain that set the stage for "the coming European war," as Hemingway put it in February 1937. After two months at the Spanish fronts, and his now highly public "conversion" to a very active antifascist, Hemingway, in fact, began to urge American intervention on the side of the Republic, writing repeatedly in *Ken* magazine that if we did not stop the fascists in Spain, we would have to fight them elsewhere.

By the time he sat down in the spring of 1939 to write *For Whom the Bell Tolls*, his prediction was coming true with a vengeance. The Spanish Republic had fallen to the fascists. Hitler had annexed Austria and dismembered and swallowed Czechoslovakia. Mussolini had invaded Albania (having already "annexed" Ethiopia in 1936). In September, when Hemingway was about half finished with the novel, Germany invaded Poland and the "coming European war" began in earnest, a war made easier by the cynical treachery of Hitler's and Stalin's nonaggression agreement only days before. That is the larger context of *For Whom the Bell Tolls*, a context Hemingway perhaps had best described a year before in a letter to his editor and good friend Max Perkins as a "carnival of treachery and rotten-ness" (*Letters*, 474).

The writer's problem, Hemingway's problem, just as he had expressed it that night in New York in 1937, was how to make the reader experience the larger truth—including now the carnival of treachery and rottenness and the lie of fascism—he knew to be contained within the specifics of the bloody Spanish conflict. And how to achieve that reader awareness without engaging in partisan politics of any kind, or perhaps by appealing to some larger partisanship, which biographer Carlos Baker has described as, "partisanship . . . in the cause of humanity."[2]

Early in the novel, Robert Jordan, resenting his "bad orders" to blow the bridge, nevertheless thinks " . . . that bridge can be the point on which the future of the human race can turn."[3] Then he admits to himself that "it can [turn] on everything that happens in this war." Finally, becoming self-conscious, he tells himself in typical fashion: "Stop worrying, you windy bastard" (43).

Robert Jordan, the Spanish professor and demolition expert, makes fun of himself (somewhat atypically for a professor perhaps), but Hemingway has made his point. Just before blowing the bridge 400 pages later, Jordan thinks, "Today is only one day in all the days that will ever be. But what will happen in all the other days that ever come can depend on what you do today" (432).

Is Robert Jordan exaggerating the blowing of the bridge? In September 1990, on the fiftieth anniversary of *For Whom the Bell Tolls*, seven Americans who had written on Hemingway went to the Gorki Institute in Moscow to participate in a commemorative conference with a dozen of our Russian counterparts. One of the questions raised early on was whether Robert Jordan had died in vain. The answer I gave our Russian colleagues then is my answer here, a figurative answer that I hope helps us understand why Hemingway originally wrote *For Whom the Bell Tolls* and provides us with the context for reading it fifty years later: "If Robert Jordan had died in vain—if the fate of humanity had not swung on that bridge and on all such bridges and on all such Robert Jordans—we would not be discussing this novel freely together here in Moscow today."

2

The Importance of the Work:
No Man Is an Island

Robert W. Lewis, third president of the Hemingway Society, and I were preparing to go to Cuba to discuss with Cuban officials the possibility of holding an international Hemingway conference in Havana. At the same time (December 1988) the then Soviet President Mikhail Gorbachev, also on his way to Cuba, stopped in New York to address the United Nations. He opened his historic address by "invoking the great English poet, John Donne, cited in his novel by Ernest Hemingway, 'No man is an island. . . . '"

What an appropriate beginning, I thought. "No man is an island": John Donne: Ernest Hemingway: Mikhail Gorbachev. England: Spain: The United States: The Soviet Union. Had Carlos Baker been alive to hear that invocation, I am sure it would have appealed greatly to him. Were not these ever-widening gyres precisely what Professor Baker had meant by the partisanship of humanity? It is one thing to cite John Donne's "Meditation," but an altogether larger issue to invoke Donne as invoked by Hemingway, invoked in turn by Mr. Gorbachev in his historic, bridge-building address.

Hemingway, not incidentally, is one of the most popular serious foreign writers of fiction in the Commonwealth of Independent States. Only Jack London's popular tales of the North Country, for obvious reasons of affinity, are more widely read. When we were in Moscow, we were amazed to learn that the edition of our colleague Alexy Zverev, of *For Whom the Bell Tolls*, published in 1988 by the Pravda Press, numbered 600,000 and sold out at once. Russian students at that time read *The Old Man and the Sea* and *For Whom the Bell Tolls* in secondary school.

Another colleague, H. R. Stoneback, who taught Hemingway and Faulkner on a Fulbright professorship in China, reports that Hemingway is by far the most popular foreign writer there. In 1987 I spent five weeks lecturing on Hemingway in Mexico, El Salvador, Venezuela, Colombia, and Chile, and I know from talking to students, professors, and writers that throughout Latin America Hemingway is the most widely read non-Spanish writer of all. Again *The Old Man and the Sea*, set in Cuba, and *For Whom the Bell Tolls*, set in Spain, are the best-known works.

In Cuba Hemingway is virtually revered, and his house in San Francisco de Paula, outside Havana, is treated almost like a shrine. In the square at Cojímar, the little fishing village of *The Old Man and the Sea*, there is a bronze bust of Hemingway. And in Pamplona, Spain, where the running of the bulls through the streets takes place every year in July just as in *The Sun Also Rises*, there is another bronze bust of him right outside the *Plaza de Toros* (bullring). It is no exaggeration to say that throughout the world, Ernest Hemingway is our most widely read serious writer of fiction.

Elsewhere I have written that *The Sun Also Rises* is Hemingway's "first, finest and most profound novel."[1] I continue to believe that it is indeed a fine and profound book and one of the most extraordinary and influential first novels ever written. But Mr. Gorbachev's citation and our visit to the then teetering Soviet Union on the eve of the collapse of communism have made me look at *For Whom the Bell Tolls* in a new light. If *The Sun Also Rises* is a novel of disintegration and fall from grace, *For Whom the Bell Tolls*, by contrast, is a novel of integration and grace regained. In the long run, the positive nature of *For Whom the Bell*

Tolls, the idea that, in fact, no man is an island and that we are all "involved in Mankinde," as John Donne wrote it, may make it Hemingway's most enduring book. In any case, Robert Jordan's unmitigated battle against totalitarianism as evidenced by his active antifascism and his careful eschewal of communism—which he considered at best the lesser of two evils—together with his ability to sacrifice himself for the Spanish cause and especially for the love of María, give him a classic heroism that only seems to intensify with the passage of time.

When Franco died in 1975 and democracy was restored in Spain, the Spanish Civil War finally seemed over. Today with the defeat of fascism, the death of Franco, and the apparent demise of communism, that fierce ideological and military conflict between the Left and the Right that began so symbolically and at the same time so literally on the taut bull's hide of Iberia in 1936, also finally seems over. The struggle begun there in Spain would tear the twentieth century to pieces. Half a million would die in Spain alone.

The artistic legacy of that conflict includes a variety of works ranging from graphic art and film to painting and literature in a number of languages. George Orwell's anticommunist memoir *Homage to Catalonia* comes to mind, as does André Malraux's novel *Man's Hope* or Arthur Koestler's *Darkness at Noon*. The two most important works of art are almost indisputably Picasso's starkly great painting, *Guernica*, and Hemingway's novel, *For Whom the Bell Tolls*, virtually the only Spanish Civil War novel to achieve lasting recognition in English. Both Picasso's canvas and Hemingway's text continue to be important today, and continue to be studied as masterpieces, partly because in each case the individual artistry outweighed the ideological concerns.

In the final analysis, it was precisely Hemingway's ability to disassociate himself and his character Robert Jordan from immediate events and his ability to write a great story about Robert Jordan and María that compel us to read the novel. Long after the politics and the particulars of the war itself are forgotten, readers will still be moved by the story of Robert Jordan and María and the band of guerrillas who attempt to blow a bridge on which the future of the human race could turn.

3

Critical Reception: Here Is a Mountain

Not long after Hemingway's speech to the Writers' Congress in New York, the critic Cyril Connolly predicted in the *New Statesman and Nation*: "Hemingway . . . is obviously the person who can write the great book about the Spanish War" (Baker 1972, 223). He was, you might say, expected to write a great novel about the Spanish Civil War a full three years before the novel's publication.

Hemingway seems to have understood his responsibility, or perhaps I should say his opportunity. "Really will have quite a lot to write when this all over. Am very careful to remember and not waste it in dispatches," he wrote to his editor Max Perkins on 5 May 1938. "When finished am going to settle down and write and the pricks and fakers like Malraux who pulled out in February 1937 to write gigantic masterpisses before it really started will have a good lesson when write ordinary sized book with the old stuff unfaked in it" (*Letters*, 467). Hemingway clearly resented André Malraux's novel *Man's Hope*, which he seemed to think was opportunistic and much too quickly done. (Ironically, however, *For Whom the Bell Tolls* turned out considerably longer than Malraux's novel.)

When he did settle down and write, he did so with full knowledge of what he was about. Begging out of a fishing tournament, he wrote to his good friend Tommy Shevlin on 4 April 1939 that the novel " . . . is the most important thing I've ever done and it is the place in my career as a writer I have to write a real one" (*Letters*, 484). Explaining the situation to his publisher Charles Scribner in a letter of 23 May 1939, he maintained that he could not interrupt the book and that he was "going to stay in one damned place until I finish this even if I go broke and lose all my friends" (*Letters*, 486).

A year and a half more of hard work, mostly in one place, went by before Hemingway's longest book was published. When it did appear on 21 October 1940, it was to overwhelmingly positive reviews—hundreds of them all across the country—especially for a writer as controversial as Hemingway had become.

The reviewer for *Newsweek* (21 October 1940), expressed the sense of expectation and fulfillment perfectly:

> Of the writers who saw the Spanish War at firsthand, probably more was expected from Ernest Hemingway than from any other. Because he knew and loved Spain and her people out of an intimacy long antedating the revolt, because he had found in the cause of the Spanish republic something to believe in and fight for, and, finally, because he is one of the great writers of our time, most people felt that the novel he would inevitably write, in his own good time, would be *the* book about the Spanish war. *For Whom the Bell Tolls*, published this week, is undoubtedly that book.

News stories about Hemingway, who was always "good copy," increased the sense of expectation that existed. For example, Robert van Gelder in an interview-piece in the *New York Times* on 11 August 1940, portrayed Hemingway as holed up in the Hotel Barclay, heroically reading proof at the exaggerated rate of 300 pages a day in the middle of a heat wave. Hemingway predicts, "The fight in Spain will have to be fought again," and then talks about his novels: "I don't know how many more I'll do. But they say that when you're in your forties you ought to know enough and have enough stuff to do one good one. I think this is it."

Ben Burns, hearing about the novel early, wrote in the San Francisco *People's World* on 23 May 1940, that Scribner's advance announcement of the publication of *For Whom the Bell Tolls* "becomes the biggest book news of the year."

And it was not just New York and San Francisco. On 11 May 1940 in the Gastonia, North Carolina, *Gazette*, notice appeared of the receipt of the manuscript at Scribner's with "all but the final chapters on which he is now at work in Cuba." Similar notices appeared all over the country, obviously from a syndicated release. But the release is not the point; the point is that Hemingway's new novel was considered newsworthy in Gastonia and in Akron, Ohio, and in Burlington, Vermont, months before it appeared.

The *Saturday Review of Literature* (26 October 1940) featured on its cover the now famous photograph of Hemingway pecking away at his trusty portable Smith-Corona as he worked on the novel in Sun Valley. The caption solemnly read, "Ernest Hemingway disappears, and in his place is the sorrowful majesty of a cause in which he believed . . . the cause of Humanity." Inside, Howard Mumford Jones called it "probably one of the finest and richest novels of the last decade," and thought that "Hemingway has done for the Spanish Civil War the sort of thing that Tolstoy did for the Napoleonic campaigns in *War and Peace*." Pilar and the other survivors at the end joined the immortals: "Their ride up the mountain is like riding into Valhalla."

On publication day, Ralph Thompson wrote in the *New York Times*, "It is the most moving document to date on the Spanish Civil War, and the first major novel of the Second World War." And he nailed down Hemingway's message: "The tragedy is present and only too plain; the bell that began tolling in Madrid four years ago is audible everywhere today."

The day before in the *New York Times Book Review*, J. Donald Adams opened his review with these words: "This is the best book Ernest Hemingway has written, the fullest, the deepest, the truest. It will, I think, be one of the major novels in American literature."

Adams believed that "it is not a depressing but an uplifting book. It has the purging quality that lies in the presenting of tragic but profound truth. Hemingway has freed himself from the negation that held him in his other novels." The massacre in Pablo's town "has the thrust and power of one of the more terrible of Goya's pictures." He concluded that, after the hunting stories, "Hemingway had found bigger game than the kudu and the lion. The hunter is home from the hill."

Throughout the country positive reviews continued to appear. Ruth Hard Bonner, writing in the Brattleboro, Vermont, *Reformer* on 30 November 1940, was "still too much moved to put things down properly in words." In the Milwaukee, Wisconsin, *Post* (14 November 1940) the anonymous reviewer stated, "There are some books which, once read, become forever part of one's experience. Such a book is Hemingway's novel of the Spanish Civil War." That reviewer also thought "the love scenes are among the most beautiful in all prose."

In the *Boston Evening Transcript* (2 November 1940), Mildred Boie wrote that María was "no literary creation; this is a creature made out of deep and sincere understanding of what love and simple beauty are. She is the poetry of the book and her being brings with it the prose-poetry that so surprisingly but fittingly distinguish the writing of the book."

Naomi Bender in the *Miami Herald* (3 November 1940) was glad "to see that the critics, who once vied with each other to see how many insults they could heap on author Ernest Hemingway, are now crawling over each other in their haste to acclaim his latest novel." On the same day in the rival Miami *News*, the nameless reviewer wrote, "It will probably be one of the major novels in American literature." And so it went, for the most part, praise heaped upon praise.

My favorite review of the novel came from the inimitable Dorothy Parker. Here are choice excerpts from her short, witty, no-nonsense review of 20 October 1940 published in the New York *PM*: "This is a book, not of three days, but of all time." She called it "beyond all comparison, Ernest Hemingway's finest book. It is not necessary politely to introduce that statement by the words 'I think.' It is so, and that is all there is to it. It is not written in his staccato manner. The pack of little Hemingways who ran along after his old style cannot hope to copy the swell and flow of his new one." On love and excitement she remarked, "But nobody can write as Ernest Hemingway can of a man and a woman together, their completion and their fulfillment. And nobody can make melodrama as Ernest Hemingway can, nobody else can get such excitement upon a printed page." Finally she claimed without the slightest hesitation, "I think that what you do about this book of Ernest Hemingway's is point to it and say, 'Here is a book.' As you would stand below Everest and say, 'Here is a mountain.'"

For Whom the Bell Tolls, chosen as a Book of the Month Club main selection, broke sales records, and the sales records in turn became news, hitting the 500,000 mark by February. Not only did Hemingway sell, but John Donne, whose "Meditation" Hemingway had used for his epigraph and title, experienced brief best-seller status over 300 years after his death. As if to top all this, Paramount paid a record price—$136,000 is the figure most often cited—for the film rights, and that in turn made more news. Hemingway's novel, serious fiction and a guaranteed page-turner at the same time, was an unprecedented success.

Not everyone was happy, of course. Mary Northrup complained loudly in the *Charlotte News* (17 November 1940) that the novel read like the "libretto of an opera. Great tragedy, great love, great character, great weakness, and a large measure of unreality." For her the characters "might as well have been Choctaw as Spanish."

The most serious criticism came, to no one's surprise, from the most serious critics. Edmund Wilson wrote a long review for the *New Republic* (28 October 1940), in which he welcomed back Hemingway, the artist. He also liked Hemingway's political depictions: "The whole picture of the Russians and their followers in Spain—which will put the *New Masses* to the trouble of immediately denouncing a former favorite at a time when they are already working overtime with so many other denunciations on their hands—looks absolutely authentic." Wilson thought Hemingway's "sense of terrain" was highly developed but thought that the novel was too long, that it was "a love story that is headed straight for Hollywood," and that the affair between

Robert Jordan and María had "the too-perfect felicity of a youthful erotic dream."

The *Partisan Review* ran two pieces in the January 1941 issue, one by Dwight Macdonald and the other by Lionel Trilling. Macdonald found it "disappointing," and the more he read "the more of a let-down" he felt. He thought the author was "floundering around, uncertain of his values and intentions, unable to come up to the pretensions of the theme." He did not think it was "a novel at all, but rather a series of short stories," which were "imbedded in a mixture of sentimental love scenes, too much talk, rambling narrative sequences, and rather dull interior monologues by Jordan." Robert Jordan himself was "simply a mouthpiece for the author" and was "a sort of Hemingwayesque scoutmaster leading his little troop of peasants." The author himself was "Hemingway with a hangover." The novel "is a political novel," but it fails "because Hemingway lacks the moral and intellectual equipment to handle such a theme." At one point Macdonald asks, "But what can be more fruitless than to follow through some five hundred pages the thoughts of a hero who has renounced thought?" The intentionally supercilious critic should never leave himself so open.

Trilling is more positive at times, comparing Hemingway to Tolstoy and saying that a restored Hemingway is "writing to the top of his bent." But Trilling is equally misguided, especially when he tells us that "when the reading is behind us what we remember is a series of brilliant scenes and a sense of having been almost constantly excited, but we do not remember a general significance." We don't? Trilling is at his most wrongheaded when he tries to tell us that Robert Jordan's death "is devastatingly meaningless," and that the overall result "is a novel which, undertaking to celebrate the community of men, actually glorifies the isolation of the individual ego."

Mark Schorer in the *Kenyon Review* (Winter 1941) wrote a far more perceptive essay, one which was almost exactly the reverse of Trilling's: "No one would seriously contend, I think, that the very motive of *For Whom the Bell Tolls* is not a tremendous sense of man's dignity and worth, an urgent awareness of the necessity of man's freedom, a nearly poetic realization of man's *collective* virtues. Indeed the individual vanishes in the political whole, but vanishes precisely to defend his dignity, his freedom, his virtue." Schorer also believed that "Hemingway's title portends nothing more than that which we have all known: that the doom of Republican Spain was our doom."

Looking back on the reviews, we can see that Schorer and the book reviewers in general were more perceptive and more in agreement than certain prominent literary essayists, especially regarding the novel's effect on its readers. As Frank L. Dennis wrote poignantly in the *Washington Post* (27 October 1940), "When you have finished it you have something to remember that will be of use to you as long as you have decisions of principle to make." This perceptive review ended with this thought: "So you are well aware, when you come to the end of this story, that when Robert Jordan lies injured and alone on a sunny Spanish hillside, waiting for the enemy to finish him, that he is about to die for you as well as for himself."

One of the very best summations—among my favorites because it speaks directly to readers today—is from Joseph Henry Jackson, the book editor of the *San Francisco Chronicle* (27 October 1940), who wrote that you could not forget the "hundreds of brief, sharp scenes that come together to make the whole. Nor will you forget the total effect of the book. As a picture of today's kind of warfare its impact is tremendous. As a story of men against death, it is convincing to the last detail. As a reminder that the bell indeed tolls for us all, and perhaps even unto the third and fourth generation, it is a grim and (I believe) completely realistic prophecy."

The most strident criticism of *For Whom the Bell Tolls* came from the veterans of the Abraham Lincoln Battalion, as the some 3,000 American volunteers who fought for the Republic in the Spanish Civil War were usually known. The opening salvo of protest was a denunciatory review in the *New Masses* (5 November 1940) by Alvah Bessie, who was a writer as well as a veteran and had known Hemingway in Spain. Bessie's lengthy major concerns were that Hemingway's novel distorted the war by "morbid concentration upon the meaning of *individual* death, *personal* happiness, *personal* misery, *personal* significance in living . . . "; that Hemingway made "the role of the Soviet Union in Spain [seem] sinister and reprehensible"; that he slandered André Marty, the organizer of the International Brigades; that he unintentionally wrote "a *Cosmopolitan* love story against a background of the Spanish Civil War"; and that he wrote "a book about Spain that is not about Spain at all."

Bessie—along with signatories Milton Wolff, National Commander; Fred P. Keller, Jr., New York Post Commander; and Irving Goff, Acting Secretary-Treasurer of the Veterans of the Abraham Lincoln Brigade—then wrote an open letter to Hemingway that was published in the *Daily Worker* and other papers of the Left, such as the San Francisco *People's World* (27 November 1940). It was similar in its complaints, more strident in tone, and added new charges such as the maligning of La Pasionaria, the famous communist orator, and Republican generals Lister and El Campesino. They termed his attack on Marty "unprincipled," and claimed that the novel failed to express the "basic lessons of Spain," an indictment that led to this statement: "The Spanish dead, slaughtered in a real war for democracy, rise to condemn as a false 'war for democracy' the present bloody and reactionary imperialist butchery, a war in the midst of which the Soviet Union stands now as then, as the best friend of the Spanish people and a great bulwark of peace, democracy and freedom." That bit of Stalinist propaganda out of the way, they were free to state their ultimate point: "We repudiate [*For Whom the Bell Tolls*] as a distorted portrayal of the war in Spain; as a false portrait of the American volunteers in Spain; as a slander of the Soviet Union, of the International Brigades and our leaders, and of the Spanish people; and as, objectively and in effect, an attack on the cause of peace, progress and democracy to which we are dedicated."

I quote these political statements at some length because it is necessary to remember the political virulence the novel aroused at the time of its publication if we are to understand the true significance of Hemingway's accomplishment. Hemingway is frequently accused of being politically naive, especially when such naivete furthers the critic's argument, as in the case of Dwight Macdonald's piece in the

Partisan Review. Yet as we shall see, Hemingway was decidedly not naive about politics, and Edmund Wilson had obviously been dead right about the discomfiture of the *New Masses* and company. They protested too much.

Hemingway, it turns out, knew ahead of time exactly what that reaction would be. On 27 October 1939, over a year before the novel's publication, he wrote to Max Perkins that it contained "what people with Communist Party obligations could never write, what most of them could never know or—if they knew—allow themselves to believe" (Baker 1969, 343).

In December from Sun Valley he warned Perkins specifically not to say anything to Alvah Bessie: "Those poor unfortunate bastards need all the ideology they can get and I would not want to deprive anyone of any anymore than would make cracks about religion to a nun. But Max it is a foul business and it was a foul business plenty of times in Spain too. But if you have a war you have to win it. If you lose you lose everything and your ideology won't save you" (*Letters*, 498). Although Hemingway admired Bessie's book, *Men in Battle*, published by Scribner's in 1939, he did not want Bessie and the "ideology boys," as he called them, getting wind of anything before publication. In January he again specifically warned Perkins not to show any of them the chapter of the massacre in the village (Baker 1969, 346).

Hemingway also knew absolutely that the "ideology boys" on the Left would, in fact, attack him. He even went so far as to take out a three-month subscription to *New Masses* beginning in October 1940 in order to monitor what they said.[1] In spite of the acrimony, Hemingway maintained contact and even a sense of solidarity with a number of them over the years, especially Milton Wolff. In fact, shortly after the letter appeared, he had a meeting with Joe North, the editor of the *New Masses*, Alvah Bessie, and a number of veterans of the Lincoln Battalion (or Brigade as it is sometimes called). Not much seems to have come of the meeting. Hemingway defended the novel, according to Bessie's account of the meeting, as "'the greatest book I have written,'" and told them that, "like Robert Jordan, he 'had no politics.'"[2]

Hemingway expected the attack from the Left; but what did he expect from the other side? J. N. Vaughn's review for *Commonweal* (13 December 1940) suggested that readers read only pages 96–130, the scene of the massacre in Pablo's village, where "The killing was done by loyalists, peasants, communists, republicans, anarchists." As for the main story, "little need be said."

Vaughn's review could be dismissed, but another blow from the Right could not. *For Whom the Bell Tolls* was not awarded the Pulitzer Prize for fiction even though board members voted it the unanimous winner. But the president of Columbia University and chairman of the prize board, Dr. Nicholas Murray Butler, vetoed Hemingway's novel, so the prize was not awarded that year.

Judgments and assessments of *For Whom the Bell Tolls* in the intervening fifty years span the entire spectrum of critical opinion. The bibliography on Hemingway and his works is long past the stage where you can expect to read it all because the number of articles and books being produced by what is not so facetiously called "The Hemingway Industry" is increasing every year. The bibliography now runs to three volumes and more than 1,200 pages (see Hanneman and Larson entries in the Selected Bibliography).

Although less has been written about *For Whom the Bell Tolls* than about *The Sun Also Rises* or *A Farewell to Arms*—largely I think because of the political and historical problems involved—the bibliography is nevertheless daunting, and it would be impossible even to outline it here. Instead I shall refer to certain important studies in what follows and for now simply say that historically the best balanced major piece on the novel is probably still Carlos Baker's chapter "The Spanish Tragedy" from *Hemingway: The Writer as Artist*, which was first published in 1952 and has been through four editions, the fourth being the 1972 edition I have previously cited. Professor Baker separated the artist from the man, successfully walked the political tightrope without falling off on the Left or on the Right, and read the novel—above and beyond politics and partisanship—as the tragedy of Spain, the greater and lesser concentricities of which touch us all. It was, Baker thought, Hemingway's best novel (Baker 1972, 116).

4

Spain: The Undiscovered Country

To understand why Hemingway wrote *For Whom the Bell Tolls* and what it meant to him, we have to understand something about Hemingway's relation to Spain. As he told Malcolm Cowley years later, "But it wasn't just the civil war I put into it . . . it was everything I had learned about Spain for eighteen years."[1]

Robert Jordan, who as we will see has some of Hemingway's own attributes, has himself written a book about Spain and "put in it what he had discovered about Spain in ten years of travelling in it, on foot, in third-class carriages, by bus, on horse- and mule-back and in trucks. He knew the Basque country, Navarre, Aragon, Galicia, the two Castiles and Estremadura well" (248). Jordan's ten years parallel Hemingway's eighteen. Although Jordan's book (we never find out the title) has been only a modest success, Jordan's and Hemingway's love for the country and for the Spanish Republic are virtually identical. For both, Spain is not simply a good country; it is a good country and the source of their writing as well.

Hemingway became interested in the Spanish art of *toreo* before he spent time in Spain and even wrote a short piece on toreo before he actually saw a corrida, taking his description from what the painter

Mike Strater had told him (Baker 1969, 108). (I will use the terms *toreo* and *corrida* throughout since "bullfighting" and "bullfight," Hemingway's use of the terms notwithstanding, are inaccurate.) Then in May and June 1923 he made his first extended trip to Spain, specifically to see corridas and learn about the art of toreo. He and Hadley returned in July, on the advice of Gertrude Stein, to attend the festival of San Fermín in Pamplona. Afterwards he wrote to a close friend, "Spain is the very best country of all. It's unspoiled and unbelievably tough and wonderful" (*Letters*, 107).

As early as the spring of 1925, before writing *The Sun Also Rises*, Hemingway had in mind writing a grand book about the bulls. As he wrote to his editor Max Perkins, "I hope some day to have [a book about] the Bull Ring, a very big book with some wonderful pictures" (*Letters*, 156). A year and a half later he wrote,

> I will keep the bull fight book going. . . . It is a long one to write because it is not to be just a history and text book or apologia for bull fighting—but instead, if possible, bull fighting its-self. . . . It might be interesting to people because nobody knows anything about it—and it really is terribly interesting—being a matter of life and death. . . . I think a really true book if it were fairly well written about the one thing that has, with the exception of the church, come down to us intact from the old days would have a certain permanent value. (*Letters*, 236–37)

Hemingway would finally finish the big book about the bulls in 1932, and it would be called *Death in the Afternoon*. Years later he would tell his son Gregory it was the most difficult book he ever wrote.[2]

What did the bulls—the *fiesta* as the Spanish people call it—mean to Hemingway? Just as war, hunting, fishing, and writing did, toreo literally fascinated him. The bullring supplied a dimension of truth. It was, according to the second page of *Death in the Afternoon*, "The only place where you could see life and death, i.e. violent death, now that the wars were over." It also provided a "certain definite action which would give me the feeling of life and death I was working for."[3] And it had the powerful attraction for Hemingway of being a beautiful, ritual spectacle that had survived from antiquity. Nowhere was "grace under pressure"—that quality he so avidly sought—more evident (*Letters*, 200).

Carlos Baker made the point that if you come to *For Whom the Bell Tolls* fresh from *Death in the Afternoon*, you will see "how much of the old Spain has been transferred out of the manual and into the novel, always with a gain in dramatic intensity." Baker believed that *Death in the Afternoon* served "as a kind of sourcebook for *For Whom the Bell Tolls*." And he thought that a reading of it was "indispensable" for understanding how Hemingway's fiction developed. It served to "illuminate the study of *For Whom the Bell Tolls*" and was important for "the light it throws on the esthetics of tragedy in Hemingway" (Baker 1972, 148–49).

The last chapter of *Death in the Afternoon*—which begins, "If I could have made this enough of a book it would have had everything in it" (*DIA*, 270) and goes on to catalog nostalgically some of the things left out—made it clear that the real subject of the book was not just toreo but Hemingway's discovery of Spain and the Spanish way of life that were best exemplified in toreo.

Hemingway went to Spain in 1937 as a writer against fascism. Robert Jordan went as a fighter against fascism. But had they both not discovered Spain prior to that, had Spain not already existed for both of them as a country worth fighting for, and a place, in Robert Jordan's case surely, and in Hemingway's case to some extent (he certainly took plenty of risks while there), worth dying for, *For Whom the Bell Tolls* would never have been written. Had the great conflict between the European powers started first in Poland, Hemingway would never have gone; neither by extension would Jordan. When the Italians began a fascist war in Ethiopia, it never occurred to Hemingway to go. But Spain—Hemingway's undiscovered country—was different. Spain, the country he, as a writer, had himself discovered, was sacred ground. As Carlos Baker wisely wrote, "The driving emotion behind *For Whom the Bell Tolls* is Hemingway's sense of the betrayal of the Spanish people" (Baker 1972, 239).

5

Politics: Discovery and Abandonment

Let's begin by reviewing Hemingway's Spanish Civil War activity, bearing in mind that the Spanish Civil War was the subject Hemingway treated most extensively. In 1937 he worked on the narration for the pro-Republican propaganda film, *Spain in Flames*. Then in Spain he helped Joris Ivens and his crew with the filming of *The Spanish Earth*, for which he later wrote the narration and for which he replaced Orson Wells as narrator. He addressed the Writers Congress in New York, then showed *The Spanish Earth* at the White House, where he said the food was "the worst I've ever eaten. . . . We had a rainwater soup followed by rubber squab, a nice wilted salad and a cake some admirer had brought in" (*Letters*, 460). He showed the film again at Frederic March's house in Hollywood to help raise $20,000 for ambulances for the Spanish Republic (in those days that meant about twenty ambulances). He became a war correspondent for the North American Newspaper Alliance (NANA); wrote pieces about the war for the *New Masses*, *Ken*, and *Verve*, and wrote his only play, *The Fifth Column*. He even wrote a piece for the Russian newspaper *Pravda*. Finally, he also did a series of short stories on the subject.

All this material about the war was written during the war. Just as the conflict was ending in March 1939, Hemingway began work on *For Whom the Bell Tolls*. Now, here's the curious part: All the material done during the war is more or less overtly political in nature, while *For Whom the Bell Tolls* is by contrast frequently apolitical. Unless we understand how and why that is true, we cannot fully understand the complexity nor even some of the beauty of *For Whom the Bell Tolls*.

Too many critics have written that Hemingway was politically naive. Dwight Macdonald's classic line (already cited) that *For Whom the Bell Tolls* was "a political novel" that was "a failure because Hemingway lacks the moral and intellectual equipment to handle such a theme," is typical of the wrongheadedness of such criticism. Hemingway did not, in fact, lack either the moral or the intellectual equipment, but he was often selective about what he wrote even early on.

Consider the following selection of comments and predictions, and notice the early dates. On 27 January 1923 in the *Toronto Star*, Hemingway called Mussolini "the biggest bluff in Europe," and then proceeded to satirize him: "There is something wrong, even histrionically, with a man who wears white spats with a black shirt."[1]

In a 1933 letter to his mother-in-law, he stated, "I hate Hitler because he is working for one thing: war. He says one thing with his mouth and does another with his hands. War is the health of the State and anyone with his conception of the state has to have war or the threat of war to keep it going" (*Letters*, 398). Does that sound naive, especially considering that it came six years before Hitler's invasion of Poland?

In the same letter he talks about Spain: "Spain is in what they call a state of confusion. All the idealists now in power have their fingers in the pie and they have gotten down to where the plums are pretty small. When they run out of pie there will be another revolution" (*Letters*, 369). And there was another revolution three years later.

In January 1934 he wrote in a piece for *Esquire*, "The spectacle of [Spain's] governing is at present more comic than tragic; but the tragedy is very close" (*By-Line*, 146). In February 1937 Hemingway wrote to his wife's family, "This is the dress rehearsal for the inevitable

European war. . . " (*Letters*, 458). To his mother-in-law he wrote in August 1937 that if the Republic lost, " . . . Hitler and Mussolini can come in and take the minerals they need to make a European war" (*Letters*, 459). And in a piece for *Ken*, which came out on 11 August 1938, he wrote, "War is due in Europe by next summer at the latest" (*By-Line*, 291). For someone supposed to be naive, Hemingway had a pretty good crystal ball.

Aside from such perspicacity, however, there is another strain in Hemingway's thinking that we need to observe to understand his underlying ideology. I use the term ideology (perhaps temperament is a clearer term) rather than politics precisely because Hemingway's ideology was always antipolitical except for a brief period during the Spanish Civil War when he suspended his ideology in order to adopt what he considered a necessary political stance.

I will call Hemingway's ideology artistic anarchism. It is not a perfect term because Hemingway was only an anarchist in the least sense of the word; that is, he was not a bomb thrower or an advocate of the overthrow of government. He did, however, believe in the minimum of government possible, as we shall presently see, especially for aesthetic—whence my term artistic—reasons. Nor, of course, do I mean that his aesthetics were anarchistic. On the contrary, his sense of art provided the highest form of order in his life.

Most of the easily adducible evidence is in his correspondence. Exhibit A is a letter to John Dos Passos in May 1932: "I can't be a Communist because I hate tyranny and, I suppose, government. . . . I can't stand *any* bloody government I suppose. . . . No larger unit than the village can exist without things being impossible" (*Letters*, 360). In *For Whom the Bell Tolls* not even the village unit would survive; in fact, it is Pablo's village in Pilar's tale that shows how horribly cruel and vindictive even the village can be.

Exhibit B is a letter to Paul Romaine in July 1932:

> As for your hoping the Leftward Swing etc. has a very definite significance for me that is so much horseshit. I do not follow the fashions in politics, letters, religion etc. . . . There is no left and right in writing. There is only good and bad writing . . . (*Letters*, 363).

Exhibit C is again a letter to Dos Passos, in October 1932: "I suppose I am an anarchist—but it takes a while to figure out. . . . I don't believe and can't believe in too much government—no matter what good is the end. To hell with the Church when it becomes a State and the hell with the State when it becomes a church" (*Letters*, 375).

The next evidence comes from a long letter Hemingway wrote to the Russian critic Ivan Kashkin in August 1935 (Kashkin's name is used for a minor Russian character in *For Whom the Bell Tolls*). Let's examine some important excerpts:

> I cannot be a communist now because I believe in only one thing: liberty. . . . I believe in the absolute minimum of government. . . . A writer is like a Gypsy. He owes no allegiance to any government. If he is a good writer he will never like the government he lives under. His hand should be against it and its hand will always be against him. The minute anyone knows any bureaucracy well enough he will hate it. Because the minute it passes a certain size it must be unjust.

It is interesting to note that even though Hemingway was never subversive to the U.S. government, the F.B.I. kept Hemingway under surveillance from about the end of the Spanish Civil War until his death, so "its hand" was in fact "against him," as he seems almost to be predicting.

"A writer is an outlyer like a Gypsy," he repeats. And what does Hemingway believe in? "A true work of art endures forever; no matter what its politics." Art, the art of writing, is virtually Hemingway's religion: "If you believe one thing and work at it always," he told Kashkin, "as I believe in the importance of writing, you have no disillusion . . . ," as one might about politics (*Letters*, 419).

It would be difficult to overemphasize the importance of this letter. Hemingway respected Kashkin (who was also his translator into Russian), regardless of his politics, and he endeavored to tell him the truth. This is vintage Hemingway, apolitical and dedicated to writing, with "the devotion to your work and respect for it that a priest of God has for his," as he would express it many years later.[2]

Politics: Discovery and Abandonment

In January 1936 Hemingway wrote another long letter to Kashkin, at the end of which he set down what he believes and what he believed during his whole career (with one small hiatus that we will examine):

> . . . the immortality I believe in is the immortality of what you write and if your stuff lasts people write about you and if they write the same sort of shit about you when you are dead that they do when you are alive it is very silly. It is all silly as hell anyway but writing isn't silly and neither is the Gulf Stream and I wish you could go out tomorrow and see it. Am going to fish tomorrow and write the next day. (*Letters*, 432)

After the Spanish Civil War broke out, as we have seen, Hemingway at first remained somewhat hesitant. Remember the letter to Harry Sylvester, the Catholic writer from Brooklyn: "The Spanish War is a bad war, Harry, and nobody is right." At the end of that letter Hemingway told Sylvester, "Take care of yourself and don't worry about politics nor religion. And *never* mix them if you can help it. I think that's a dirty outfit in Russia now but I don't like any governments" (*Letters*, 457).

Hemingway did not always follow his own advice about not mixing politics and religion. When he married Pauline Pfeiffer in 1927, he had become formally Catholic, but now Catholic support of Franco's side caused him to break with the Church. He wrote to Pauline's mother in August 1938 that it seemed somehow "'crooked' to have anything to do with a religious institution so closely allied to fascism" (Baker 1969, 333). So in this sense he did not mix politics and religion since his politics and his religion were on opposite sides in Spain.

If we consider Hemingway's religion (with a lower case "r") to be his art, then he did indeed for a while mix the two. The civil war short stories and his play, *The Fifth Column*, show a frequent mix of them, as does the ending he added to his prewar novel *To Have and Have Not*, which was published in October 1937, after his first view of the war in Spain.

Somewhere around the beginning of the war Hemingway decided clearly which side he would actively support. The exact moment, if there was one, is unclear, but in December 1936 he told Max Perkins, "I've *got* to go to Spain" (*Letters*, 455). By January he was doing serious propaganda work for the pro-Republican film, *Spain in Flames*, and in February he joined the corporation called Contemporary Historians to work on *The Spanish Earth* with the Dutch communist Joris Ivens as director.

Hemingway's vested interest in the politics of the war, however, was not to endure. Whether because of disillusionment with political developments or simply because the Republic lost, or both, is not certain. In any case Hemingway was sick of the whole process by late 1938. "Well, we've lost another war," he lamented to Max Perkins in February 1939 (*Letters*, 478); by "another" Hemingway means first Mussolini's successful invasion of Ethiopia, and now the loss of Spain.

Yet for a while, especially in 1937, Hemingway actively supported the Spanish Republic. As he would write to critic Edmund Wilson years later, "There is no use in arguing the history of the Spanish Republic now. But it was something I believed in deeply long before it was an American Communist cause. . . . I had believed in the Republic and known the people who worked for it since the early twenties" (*Letters*, 733). Is Hemingway exaggerating? Only, I think about the "early twenties." As he wrote to Dos Passos in June 1931 from Madrid: "Been following politics closely" (*Letters*, 341).

I cannot stress enough how important Hemingway's love for Spain—a free Spain—was. He often complained that he was homesick for Spain. In March 1953, when he had been out of Spain for fifteen years, he wrote to the critic Bernard Berenson, "Everyone loves something and I love Spain and know it, in a small way . . . " (*Letters*, 812).

Martha Gellhorn, who shared so much of the Spanish Civil War experience with Hemingway would comment, "I think it was the only time in his life when he was not the most important thing there was. He really cared about the Republic and he cared about that war. I believe I never would've gotten hooked otherwise."[3]

For a brief period Hemingway had a genuine devotion to the cause of the Republic. As he put it, "the period of fighting when we thought that the Republic could win was the happiest period of our lives" (Baker 1972, 231). Hemingway spoke so eloquently at Frederic March's house in Hollywood—"of the death of such friends as Lucasz and Heilbrun [from the International Brigades], the indiscriminate bombing of civilian populations, the killing and maiming of children, and the sufferings of the troops" in order to raise money for ambulances for the Republic—that Scott Fitzgerald reported to Max Perkins that Hemingway's "attitude had 'something almost religious about it'" (Baker 1969, 316).

No, Hemingway did not follow his own advice. He mixed politics and religion, so to speak, but we must make no mistake here: that volatile mixture did not include communism as many leftist critics rather cavalierly assumed when he took up the cause of the Republic. We have already seen his rejection of communism before the war in his correspondence. He also rejected it during the war and in person. Something he told Joe North, the editor of *New Masses*, summarizes his position rather neatly: "I like Communists when they're soldiers, but when they're priests, I hate them" (Baker 1969, 330).

Hemingway's position was actually clearer than it has been made to seem by critics who assumed that because he was pro-Republican and antifascist that he was also a de facto communist, as so many were. Edmund Wilson, as Carlos Baker put it, "referred (quite erroneously) to Hemingway's Stalinism," and the reviewer for *Time* said that Hemingway "had now safely recovered from the Red rash" (Baker 1972, 237). Hemingway explained the process years later to Bernard Berenson. He is writing of the Russian journalist Mikhail Koltzov (Kharkov in *For Whom the Bell Tolls*):

> He [Koltzov] knew I was not a Communist and never would be one. But because he believed in me as a writer he tried to show me how everything was run so that I could give a true account of it. I tried to do that when I wrote the book. But I did not start on the book until *after* the Republic had lost the war and it was *over* because I would not write anything in the war which could hurt the Republic which I believed in and tried to serve as well as I could. (*Letters*, 789; my emphasis).

"I would not write anything in [during] the war which could hurt the Republic." This phrase is the crux of the matter. Hemingway never had a "Red rash," nor was he ever remotely a Stalinist. It is just that during the war—when the communists, especially the Soviets, were the only aid the Republic had—it was not feasible to criticize the Reds, the Soviets, the Russians, or the communists any more than it would have been practical to criticize the Republican generals and troops.

But once the war was over, the discipline of not writing anything that "could hurt the Republic" was no longer necessary, and Hemingway was free to write the truth. And that is exactly what he did, even to the point of criticizing in *For Whom the Bell Tolls* some of the same Republican generals he had extolled in *The Spanish Earth*.

The old Hemingway reemerged, and now, after the fact, his old artistic anarchism back intact, he could write a great novel about the war. And the interesting thing is, the more he wrote—the more he made it up—the further he moved away from the real war he had known so well and that had so disappointed him. What he was now free to write about became the background action, the setting in which the more intimate drama of Robert Jordan and the guerrillas, and especially Robert Jordan and María, could be played out.

6

The Real War: Treachery and Rotten-ness

Fed up and soured on politics, both inside Spain and in the rest of Europe, and fed up and soured on the democracies' unwillingness or inability to act (especially England and France, but also the U.S.), Hemingway vented his frustration to Arnold Gingrich, the editor of *Esquire*, from Paris in October 1938: "Things here are so foul, now, that if you think about them you go nuts. So am just writing now" (*Letters*, 473). A few days later he voiced that complaint to Max Perkins that we examined in chapter one about "the sort of let down and carnival of treachery and rotten-ness that's going on." (Hemingway is not just referring to Spain but also to the democracies' caving in as Hitler "annexed" the Sudetenland from Czechoslovakia.) He continued with some comments on his writing, " . . . it's been hard to work. But I have two Chapters done on the novel." Then he mentioned a completed Spanish Civil War story, "Night Before Battle," and remarked, "I haven't written the napoleonic story yet. But will" (*Letters*, 474).

These enigmatic fragments introduce us to one of Hemingway's most productive periods. As the enthusiasm for the cause of the Republic began to wane, Hemingway started to write a series of stories about the Spanish Civil War. Between summer 1938 and spring 1939 he finished five stories on the subject. These stories are instrumental in our understanding of *For Whom the Bell Tolls*, which may have been "the novel" mentioned to Max Perkins. (He also mentioned "two chapters done on a novel" to Gingrich.) In spite of feeling "gloomy," he told Perkins, "Writing is a hard business Max but nothing makes you feel better" (*Letters*, 474). We need to look at these stories briefly to understand why they made Hemingway feel better and to see how they led directly into the creation—literally the creation—of *For Whom the Bell Tolls*.

Although Hemingway wrote about the war as fact and as fiction, the distinction between the two is not always a simple matter. *For Whom the Bell Tolls* was, for example, mostly fiction, whereas his news dispatches were largely factual. Yet in both areas there is a crossing over of fact and fiction. Real-life figures such as André Marty, the French Commissar who was chief of the International Brigades, and a number of the general officers for the Republic—Modesto, Durán, Lister—appear in *For Whom the Bell Tolls*. On the other hand, a good deal of opinion, even political opinion or propaganda, as well as rich descriptions that read like fiction, make their way into the news dispatches.

One of the best examples of this blurring of fact and fiction is "Old Man at the Bridge." Originally cabled from Barcelona on Easter Sunday of 1938—only a few hours after the events it portrays—as a factual piece for *Ken* magazine, "Old Man at the Bridge" was subsequently published as the last "story" in *The Fifth Column and the First Forty-nine Stories*.

Hemingway was a kind of pioneer in new journalism and the nonfiction novel, as books such as *Death in the Afternoon* and *Green Hills of Africa* demonstrate, so his crossing of genre comes as no surprise. Since his self-professed method of writing, "inventing from experience," is a kind of oxymoronic negation of any absolute categories of fact and fiction in the first place, it may be more accurate to speak of the real war and the invented or imagined war in Hemingway's writings than to attempt to distinguish too closely between fact and fiction, a practice that much recent criticism has, in any case, made rather suspect.

The writing about the real war, by which I mean the Spanish Civil War as Ernest Hemingway actually viewed it, includes his political articles and war dispatches, his play *The Fifth Column*, and the short stories "The Denunciation," "The Butterfly and the Tank," "Night Before Battle," "Under the Ridge," and the recently published "Landscape with Figures." In the play and in these stories, Hemingway was writing from actual experience, and, although he was to some extent inventing from that experience, these pieces were largely crafted from events Hemingway himself took part in. He even made his own room in the Hotel Florida the setting for the play and, in part, for the story "Night Before Battle." And his favorite bar, Chicote, was the locale for "The Denunciation," "The Butterfly and the Tank," and for the beginning of "Night Before Battle." These stories of the Spanish Civil War have two characteristics in common. The first-person narrator is clearly Ernest Hemingway himself—correspondent, filmmaker, writer, raconteur, personage. There is no making himself up as in the often-autobiographical stories about Nick Adams. In fact the occasional use of a fictional name—Henry/Enrique Emmunds in "The Denunciation" and Edwin Henry in "Night Before Battle" and "Landscape with Figures"—only makes his real identity more obvious.

The second characteristic is that the real subject of all these stories is the political nature of the conflict at hand. In "The Denunciation" the narrator tells us about the bar Chicote's during the old days before the war: "A lot of people went there that I did not like, the same as at The Stork [in New York], say, but I was never in Chicote's that it wasn't pleasant. One reason was that you did not talk politics there."[1] The narrator is, of course, being ironic since, during the war, that is virtually the only subject anyone talks about, and it is the subject of this story itself.

These two characteristics plainly reveal Hemingway's increasing personal distaste for politics as the thirties and the Spanish Civil War were coming to a close. They also help us understand how and why *For Whom the Bell Tolls* would become an invented world where real

Hemingway observing the battle of the Casa de Campo in Madrid, probably from a ruined block of flats on the Paseo de Rosales he dubbed the "Old Homestead."

Courtesy of the Hemingway Collection, John F. Kennedy Library. (Photo no. EH5402P)

politics was largely a matter of Robert Jordan's remembrance of nights past at Gaylord's, hobnobbing with the Russians, or a political vendetta against the likes of André Marty, whose vicious authoritarianism was precisely the opposite of Hemingway's anarchistic temperament.

The stories formed something of a group in Hemingway's mind at the time of their composition. In February 1939, less than four months after the publication of *The Fifth Column and the First Forty-nine Stories*, he wrote to Max Perkins from Key West about the possibility of a new book of stories: "I ought to have enough new stories for a book in the fall or do you think that is too soon for another book of stories?" (*Letters*, 479). On 25 March, just as he was beginning *For Whom the Bell Tolls*, he wrote Perkins a second letter from Key West about a new story about the war that "Pauline thinks among best I've ever written, called Under the Ridge" (*Letters*, 482). In this letter he reiterates his desire to publish the stories as a group, now including "Under the Ridge": "So it looks like we will have a book of stories *and a novel*" (*Letters*, 482; my emphasis).

The project for the Civil War stories occurred to Hemingway in February and March of 1939, just as he was beginning *For Whom the Bell Tolls*. Although he would not pursue this project, the connection between the stories and the germination of the novel is important to bear in mind. They were not really separable, as the second Key West letter reveals quite vividly. In fact, it may well have been his shift from the stories to the novel at this point that precluded the project to bring out the book of stories. Swept up in the excitement of writing the novel, Hemingway surely lost enthusiasm for these stories that simply could not measure up to the big book.

At the end of that first letter to Perkins, which fairly radiates creative energy, Hemingway relates to Perkins his bad dreams about Spain: "Last night I was caught in this retreat again in the goddamndest detail. I really must have a hell of an imagination. That's why should *always* make up stories—*not* try to remember what happened" (*Letters*, 479). This sentiment echoed something Gertrude Stein had told him years before in Paris: " . . . the parts that fail are where [you] remember visually rather than make up . . . " (*Letters*, 310).

Hemingway's insistence on the importance of imagination to his fiction is a point he would reiterate in his second letter to Perkins on 25 March 1939. Instead of the stories he had originally gone to Cuba to write, he had finished "Under the Ridge" and "started on another I'd had no intention of writing for a long time and working steadily every day found I had fifteen thousand words done; that it was very exciting; and that it was a novel." The novel, of course, was *For Whom the Bell Tolls*, and Hemingway was obviously very pleased with it: "It is 20 times better than that Night Before Battle which was flat where this is rounded and recalled where this is invented" (*Letters*, 482). From this point on the novel absorbed him completely and the project to publish a book of Spanish Civil War stories disappeared from view (to be published posthumously).

For better or worse, these stories present the real war as Hemingway experienced it, an experience that included being on the losing side. Remember what he told Max Perkins in the first Key West letter: "Well, we've lost another war" (*Letters*, 478). There is no doubt Hemingway was seriously disillusioned about the state of affairs.

What these stories did, I believe, precisely because they were autobiographical and political, was to purge the real war and the real loss of the Spanish Republic from Hemingway's fiction. Perhaps nothing could really purge such a loss personally, but literarily at least he got out of his system the dreadful reality of the war as he had experienced it. The stories as a group became a kind of cathartic fictional memoir.

That catharsis opened the way for the writing of *For Whom the Bell Tolls*, which was rounded rather than flat, invented rather than recalled, and exciting—twenty times better than "Night Before Battle." Had Hemingway not written these stories, it might have taken him much longer to get to *For Whom the Bell Tolls*.

Martin Light has written that these stories "can be seen as part of Hemingway's search for a true way to recreate the Spanish experience."[2] I think they are that and more—they also readied him to write the great romantic war novel he so badly wanted to do. Remember what he wrote to Tommy Shevlin on 4 April 1939: " . . . it is the most important thing I've ever done and it is the place in my career as a writer I have to write a real one" (*Letters*, 484).

Years later, looking back, he would write to Charles Poore, "Dr. Tolstoi was at Sevastopol. But not at Borodino. He wasn't in business in those days. But he could invent from knowledge we all were at some damned Sevastopol" (*Letters*, 800). Hemingway was not at the real La Granja offensive in late May 1937 (he was in Bimini at the time), just as he had not been in the retreat from Caporetto, which he wrote about in *A Farewell to Arms*. But he knew the territory, and, as the Civil War stories show so well, he was in fact at battles such as the Casa de Campo outside Madrid and in the battle of the Jarama south of Madrid.

These stories about the Spanish Civil War—real battles in the real war—were Hemingway's Sevastopol. They show very clearly that he could write accurately and well—despite what his Spanish and American critics have said—about the war and about the politics of the war. "Under the Ridge" is a wonderful and undervalued story, one that Hemingway revealingly referred to in a letter to Charles Scribner as "warming up" for *For Whom the Bell Tolls* (*Letters*, 486). And *For Whom the Bell Tolls* was his Borodino, an attempt to create his own twentieth-century equivalent of *War and Peace*, which he told Archibald MacLeish in 1925 "is the best book I know" (*Letters*, 179). He set out to create, not just report, drawing on all the raw material of his experience in Spain and in the Spanish Civil War.

A READING

7

The Invented War: Telling a Story

"The truth is that what really interests me is telling a story."
Gabriel García Márquez

In a recent interview Colombian novelist and confessed Hemingway disciple Gabriel García Márquez talked about his novel, *Love in the Time of the Cholera*, but his remarks are equally valid for *For Whom the Bell Tolls* and, I believe, for any "period" or historical novel. "Have you ever noticed," he queries, "what Flaubert did with the distances between places in Paris? You find that the French writers have their characters take walks that are impossible. It's a poetization of space."[1]

In the novel García Márquez placed the Café de la Parroquia, which is actually located in Veracruz, Mexico, in Cartagena, Colombia. Why? Because, as he explains,

> The Café de la Parroquia *could* be in Cartagena perfectly well. The fact that it isn't is purely incidental. . . . [It] *would* be in Cartagena if the Spaniard who built it had immigrated to Cartagena instead of to Veracruz. . . . How marvelous to have the

43

freedom to be a writer who says, 'Well I'm going to put the Café de la Parroquia where I want it to be.' Every day I'm writing I say to myself how marvelous it is to *invent* life. . . . This novel isn't a historical reconstruction. Rather it contains historical elements used poetically. All writers do this. (García Márquez, 136–37; his emphasis)

I doubt that all writers use historical elements so freely, but we can safely say that Hemingway and García Márquez do. That is, they invent, and when necessary they move cafés—or bridges or battle lines—to suit their own poetic or inventive purposes.

There are, I believe, two different ways to look at *For Whom the Bell Tolls*: We can look at it as a documentary novel, that is, as a literal picture, of the Spanish Civil War; or we can consider it a novel, that is, as a work of the imagination, as an invention. The way we choose to focus on the work may well determine what our eventual critical opinion will be.

As a documentary, as a picture of the actual war, *For Whom the Bell Tolls* could be considered at least a partial failure because the picture is at least partially invented, or from a strictly historical perspective, false. That "falseness" is one reason Spanish writers such as Arturo Barea, Julio Alvarez del Vayo, and Juan Benet have taken such fierce umbrage with *For Whom the Bell Tolls*.

Barea, in 1941, was the first to point out what some of these faults were, and his main contention—the novel's failure to render the reality of the Spanish Civil War—is, I think, basically correct, at least from his point of view.[2] We now know, however, that Hemingway was capable of writing about the real war but for whatever reasons chose not to (something Barea did not know). The point is that Hemingway *intentionally* wrote an "invented" novel rather than a personal rendition of the war's reality.

An admittedly indignant Julio Alvarez del Vayo, a communist who was foreign minister of Republican Spain during the Civil War, claimed to know from personal experience that "the Spanish Civil War was fundamentally alien to [Hemingway]"; that his "was the Spain of the running of the bulls," and so forth.[3] And the preeminent Spanish

The Invented War: Telling a Story

Civil War novelist Juan Benet remarked to Martha Gellhorn and me at a Michigan State conference on the literature of the Spanish Civil War that, in his opinion, *For Whom the Bell Tolls* was more unbearable (*"insoportable"*) than the movie made from it, that its error was that it was written to be a success, that it was just cardboard figures and stereotypes, that there was no enigma in it, nothing of the human heart, that it was old-fashioned as all historical novels are. Traditional, I wondered; yes, he said, probably the most traditional of all Hemingway's books.[4]

From the point of view of the documentary novel, all these criticisms, even the exaggerations, have some merit, including the criticism (some of it my own) that, realistically speaking, the novel does not work linguistically as it should.[5] For her part, Martha Gellhorn (whose antipathy to her ex-husband is well known), added that she thought the "literally translated Spanish was awful" and said she told him so at the time.[6]

But the real question becomes, is this critical point of view valid for understanding the novel? Is it not excessively literal-minded, especially once we understand that Hemingway deliberately chose to write an "invented" novel?

Robert A. Martin, in a more balanced and positive tone, observes quite sensibly that the book is a "masterful blend of fact and fiction" and that is what gives it the "status of a classic war novel."[7] Michael J. B. Allen, who sees the war as symbolic, allegorical, and parabolic, concludes that Hemingway is a "myth maker, and it is the manifest quality of the myth rather than the accuracy of the reporting which accounts for the novel's enduring fascination."[8]

I admit that the question of fact and fiction in *For Whom the Bell Tolls* is a vexing one, a question that has troubled me and my students for years. Omniscience is part of the problem. In *The Sun Also Rises* and *A Farewell to Arms* we look through Jake Barnes's or Frederic Henry's eyes, but in *For Whom the Bell Tolls*, Hemingway-God is sometimes our guide. The first draft of the novel shows us that it began as a first-person narrative but that Hemingway quickly abandoned the forgiving limitations of single-mindedness for the difficult world of all-knowing.[9] Hemingway was clearly aware of this problem. During final editing he wrote to Max Perkins, remarking, "I don't like to write like God" (*Letters*, 515).

I do not think the problem of fact and fiction, especially as they are seen as accuracy and inaccuracy, will ever be resolved with regard to this novel. The non-believers will never be able to accept Hemingway-God's "flaws," and the Hemingway fundamentalists will continue to insist on the infallibility of his-His word.

In the long run, and now that we are beyond the fiftieth anniversary we can appropriately speak of the long run, the rawness of the so-called factual errors will probably fade, and the mythic qualities will likely assume a larger critical profile.

At the Moscow Conference we wondered whether Russian-language critics continued to look at *War and Peace* as a historically accurate novel. And we got an interesting answer.

It turns out that Tolstoy was criticized severely for the inaccuracy of military details in *War and Peace*. As our colleague Pavel Balditsin of the Gorky Institute of World Literature in Moscow informed us, there was a man named Alexandr Dragomirov, a contemporary of Tolstoy, who even wrote a book on the subject. But today, as Pavel Balditsin pointed out, we continue to read Tolstoy, but no one reads Dragomirov. And another colleague, Yekaterina Stetsenko, commented that the heated discussions *For Whom the Bell Tolls* provoked among us were proof enough of the brilliance of the novel. Perhaps, she mused, its very lack of perfection was indicative of its greatest achievement.

I am trying to arrive at a critical point of departure that affirms that *For Whom the Bell Tolls*—all of it, including the "real parts," which are couched around and within the invented foreground action—was invented.

It was invented for two reasons: 1) because Hemingway was disgusted with, had dealt with, and was through with the real war; and 2) because invention, as he often said, could be more real than reality. He was no longer interested in the ethos of the Spanish Civil War; he wanted its mythos. Juan Benet said there was nothing of the human heart in it, but it was precisely the human heart that Hemingway was after, not the realism but the romance, through word, through story, through legend, in a brave attempt to arrive at the universal particular.

Here is a modern analogy: I have never known anyone who was in the war in Vietnam who likes the film *Apocalypse Now*. But there are those of us who, not having been in the Southeast Asian conflict, think it is a brilliant film, not as a documentary but as an art film. Over the years, I have finally come to believe that understanding how Hemingway's inventive process worked—how he played out on the visualized, mental stage of his imagination the war that he created in his mind—is a higher critical question than the accuracy of his details of the actual conflict. And at this juncture there is simply no doubt about Hemingway's deep understanding of the war. In fact it was precisely from that understanding that he was able to invent.

That brings us to the fascinating question of just how much of *For Whom the Bell Tolls* is completely invented, not remembered from reality but entirely imagined, or at least so changed in the smithy of his imagination that it is not recognizable. The answer is, of course, a great deal. For our purposes, I will identify three areas for discussion that we will take up in successive chapters: setting, characters, and action. These areas are not, as we shall see, always entirely separable.

As Hemingway matured as a writer, he invented more and more. In some ways that tendency was more ambitious than his early work, but it was also more dangerous the farther he got from actual experience. It entailed more risk but also involved more mythic reverberations. For better or for worse, what seems to have interested him most in *For Whom the Bell Tolls*, all literal and factual considerations aside, was what always seems to interest the greatest writers of fiction. As García Márquez put it in the epigraph with which I began this chapter, "The truth is that what really interests me is telling a story." For Hemingway, too, telling a story was always the highest form of truth, and in *For Whom the Bell Tolls* he has told his most extended, his most ambitious, his most moving and, for many readers, his best story.

8

The Setting: The Country You Know

James Joyce, the contemporary writer Hemingway held in highest esteem, began his last great, extremely difficult novel, *Finnegans Wake* (published in its entirety in 1939 with excerpts published along the way as *Work in Progress*), with a half sentence that completes the unfinished sentence at the novel's close. This technique ties the novel into a circle like a snake swallowing its tail. Joyce had been a definite influence on Hemingway since the twenties, and Hemingway freely admitted to Arnold Gingrich in 1933 that he had learned a good deal of technical information from reading Joyce (Baker 1969, 240). Hemingway undoubtedly read at least some of *Finnegans Wake*. Regardless of the amount, he gave *For Whom the Bell Tolls* a clearly circular structure not unlike Joyce's.

This circularity is most apparent in the novel's opening: "He lay flat on the brown, pine-needled floor of the forest, his chin on his folded arms, and high overhead the wind blew in the tops of the pine trees"; and closing: "He could feel his heart beating against the pine needle floor of the forest" (1, 471). At the beginning and at the end, Jordan is lying prone on the floor of the forest, on the bosom of the Spanish earth he loved so much.

The Setting: The Country You Know

Carlos Baker has already discussed the circular nature of the plot, and we will consider that design later. Right now the circular setting of the novel is interesting to notice. The entire action of the novel takes place in three days and nights and the morning of the fourth day, almost entirely in a very limited area of the Guadarrama Mountains between Madrid and Segovia. Except for flashbacks, one short chapter (thirty-two) at Gaylord's in Madrid, and Andrés's crossing the lines to try to warn General Golz, virtually everything happens in a very small area somewhere between the pass of Navacerrada and the sawmill town of Valsaín-La Pradera (sometimes spelled Balsaín) near La Granja. Highway N-601, as it is listed today, is and was the only major road in the area and the only one with a bridge. Furthermore, this is in the general area where the historic, that is, the real, La Granja Offensive (also called the Segovia Offensive) took place in late May 1937, precisely the time indicated in the novel.

The pine-needled Spanish earth and the general description of the mountains Hemingway paints are the "realest" parts of his setting. Something he wrote to Charles Poore of the *New York Times* in 1953 catches the spirit of what I think he did as he wrote the novel in Cuba. Although he is referring to *A Farewell to Arms*, the procedure applies almost equally as well to *For Whom the Bell Tolls*: "The country you know, also the weather. Then you have a map 1/50,000 for the whole front or sector; 1/5,000 if you can get one for close. Then you invent from other people's experience and knowledge and what you know yourself" (*Letters*, 800).

I do not mean that Hemingway necessarily needed to use a detailed map of the terrain here. The important phrases are rather "The *country* you know, also the *weather*. . . . Then you *invent*. . . . " The weather, the high wind in the pines, the possibility of snow in May, the country with its mountain streams, the high meadows with heather and gorse, and the needled pine forests with the brown trunks of the trees—those Hemingway already knew well, and he got them exactly right.

After all, he had spent, as he put it in a news dispatch dated 30 April 1937, "a hard ten days visiting four central fronts, including all high positions, hours on horseback, and climbing to important positions 4,800-feet high in the Guadarrama Mountains, which, with the snows melted, can be studied intelligently."[1] William Braasch Watson comments on this dispatch: "As for his inspection trip into the mountains with Martha Gellhorn, perhaps it was, as Hemingway depicted it here, 'a hard ten days,' but some of the scenes later included in *For Whom the Bell Tolls* suggest that gathering military intelligence was not its sole objective" (Watson 1988, 36–37). At any rate, he did get the splendid country and the weather as they really are.

The bridge and the cave, however, are another matter. Certain biographers of Hemingway threw everyone off the track to begin with by reporting they had actually seen them. A. E. Hotchner was first in 1966, when he quoted Hemingway as having answered a question in Madrid in 1954 about how much of the book was real. Hemingway supposedly said, "Not as much as you may think. There was the bridge that was blown, and I had seen that. The blowing of the train as described in the book was also a true event."[2] As we will see in the last chapter, Hemingway's statements may not be as farfetched as they sound. For our purposes here, however, it is sufficient to note that no such events took place in this sector of the war, and that if Hemingway did make such statements, he was hiding at least as much as he was revealing.

Hotchner further complicated matters by reporting that the following occurred in 1956: "Ernest showed me the cold mountain stream where Pilar had washed her feet, the cave where Pablo's band lived, the bridge since rebuilt, that was the target of the book" (Hotchner, 182). Hotchner also includes two photographs, one of a picnic "where the main action of *For Whom the Bell Tolls* occurred," and the other of "Ernest at the cold mountain stream where Pilar washed her feet" (Hotchner, between 146–47).

Then Mary Hemingway in her autobiography, *How It Was*, added this description from 1953:

> Below the road on our right a clear, fast stream, the Río Eresma, rushed under a small stone bridge. It was the forest of *For Whom the Bell Tolls*. Through the treetops we could glimpse a high barren hilltop, where Sordo had his fight, and we saw that new

Hemingway at the Eresma River, a little downstream from the bridge site, probably in 1956. This photo, most likely by Mary Hemingway or A. E. Hotchner, was made the same day that Hotchner reported a picnic at the place where Pilar washed her feet.

Courtesy of the Hemingway Collection, John F. Kennedy Library. (Photo no. EH 24405)

stones in the bridge filled the apex of the arch. Ernest murmured, "Now I am glad to see it is like how I wrote it," happy if ungrammatical. "We held the tops of all this along here. They were about three-quarters of the way down on the road you see to the right. In some places the two lines were less than ten meters apart."[3]

Sounds clear enough, right? The Eresma River is identified, just as we should have supposed, since it is the only river with a bridge on a main road between Valsaín or La Granja and Navacerrada. Hotchner remembers seeing the cave. Mary Hemingway remembers Hemingway remembering everything right down to the battle lines. She even remembers Hemingway's remembering "like how" he wrote it from thousands of miles away: "I am glad to see it is like how I wrote it." But, as Hemingway wrote in *Death in the Afternoon* twenty years prior to his reputed remark, "Memory, of course, is never true" (*DIA*, 100). In other words, welcome to the wonderful world of Hemingway biography.

We can clear this up with a little modern detective work. Although I had been in this area many times, beginning in 1963, I had never actually searched for concrete evidence of *For Whom the Bell Tolls* until I decided to write this book. At that point, however, I determined to try to get hard evidence on a few subjects.

The first thing was to ask my friend Thomas Entwhistle, a fine student of the Spanish Civil War, who was then (1988) at the Center of International Studies in Madrid, to take me over the battleground itself. Somewhat to my surprise we whizzed past the bridge, headed down through the narrows on the river, and kept on going down toward and finally into Valsaín. "Tomás," I protested, "where are we going?" "You want to see the battleground, don't you?" he replied, pointing into the center of Valsaín.

It turns out the actual battle took place down around a series of outcroppings on either side of Valsaín. The bridge, known as the Puente de la Cantina, or Puente del Peñón, is back up at kilómetro 67 (on the military map; the stone road markers above and below the bridge read 131 and 130), and Valsaín is down at kilómetro 74, a good four miles down beyond the bridge. In other words, had the action been real instead of invented by Hemingway—who was, we should remember, biographical remarks notwithstanding, not even in Spain but in Bimini at the time—the guerrillas would have been sense-lessly blowing a bridge behind their own lines, and they would not have been operating in enemy territory at all.

The lines prior to the offensive, which began on 30 May 1937, were somewhat ill-defined, but at no time was the bridge *behind* the Nationalist (enemy) lines. The placement of the lines was Hemingway's invention, possibly some reflection of his horseback trip from the month before, or, more likely, simply a fictional necessity.

The real offensive, which was led by "General Walter" (his real name was Karol Swierczweski), the model for Hemingway's General Golz, did indeed fail, and its failure, according to historian Hugh Thomas, "sealed the fate of Bilbao."[4] Bilbao, the industrialized capital of the Basque country, was considered the key to the war in the north, which is to say that the failed offensive actually was one of the turning points, perhaps the primary turning point, of the war. But the guerrilla action itself was all Hemingway's invention.

In fact the guerrillas themselves in that sector seem to have been an invention. In 1989 I returned to the *For Whom the Bell Tolls* country to get to know better the whole landscape where the invented action took place. The first place I went was to the *Instituto para la Conservación de la Naturaleza* (Institute for the Conservation of Nature) office at the sawmill in La Pradera (ICONA is on the order of U.S. National Forests). ICONA is in charge of all the timberland in this area, an area which is still known as the finest stand of wild or natural pines in Spain.

On 20 July, I spoke at some length with the *ingeniero técnico* (technical engineer) in charge of the ICONA station, Sr. Javier Donés Pastor. Among the many interesting things he told me, three stand out for our purposes. First, that the sawmill at La Pradera (on some maps, Pradera de Navalhorno) is the only one and that there never was one up by the bridge; so Hemingway evidently invented that too. Second, that the entire area is granite and consequently there are no caves any-where in it. And third, that there were no guerrillas working in this area, in caves or out of them, during the Spanish Civil War.

I asked him about La Cueva del Monje (The Cave of the Monk), a name on the 1:50,000 military map of the area, on the northwestern flank of (Mt.) Peñalara, not far from the bridge. Its name and location seemed perfect, and part of the Loyalist offensive had actually begun there. "It's not a cave," he told me, "just an outcropping of stone shaped something like a dolmen." Then he did something very generous. He called in two of his senior *guardas forestales* (forest rangers) and put them and their Land Rover at my disposal for as long as I needed.

I spent the rest of the day with guardas Venancio González and Gregorio Cobos, both of whom had spent most of their lives there and both of whom were experts in this terrain. We went to La Cueva del Monje, which is not a cave at all, only a big slab of rock that from a certain distance suggests the mouth of a cave. Popular names in Spain are frequently misleading, tending to exaggerate an aspect for poetic reasons rather than for topographic accuracy.

The guardas assured me that there simply are no caves anywhere in the area, but we saw an impressive stand of forest—huge pines with brown trunks—wild cattle and horses among the trees, glades and meadows with heather and gorse, thick green wild grass and blood red poppies. We finished our tour not far above the bridge, at about kilómetro 66 1/2 (between road markers 133 and 132) where the *camino forestal* (the forest road) joins N–601, an ideal place to begin a walk into this splendid country. Nothing makes the story come alive like experiencing the actual location.

Others I talked to around Valsaín confirmed that there were no guerrilla actions in that area. For example, Francisco Muñoz, in his seventies, who was born in La Pradera and whose father led people back and forth between the lines, assured me there had been no guerrilla actions in this sector—none whatsoever.

The bridge itself has caused a good deal of interesting speculation. Not only did Hemingway certainly seem to identify the Cantina Bridge as the bridge in question, the real bridge, that is, but there seems to exist no other bridge in contention. And here we should qualify by saying no other bridge *site* in contention, because the stone bridge over the Eresma River, the one apparently identified by Mary

Hemingway, Hemingway himself, and Hotchner (whose photographs were clearly on the Eresma), could not possibly be confused with the bridge in the novel.

The first time the bridge appears in the novel—Jordan had previously "walked over it on his way to La Granja on a walking trip in 1933" (4), just as Hemingway himself had done the same year on a hunting trip with his friend Luis Quintanilla[5]—it is described in the following terms:

> It was a *steel* bridge of a single span and there was a sentry box at each end. It was wide enough for two motor cars to pass and it spanned, in solid-flung *metal* grace, a *deep gorge* at the bottom of which, *far below*, a brook leaped in white water through rocks and boulders down to the main stream of the pass (35; my emphasis).

The situation of the bridge on a small white-water stream leading to the main body of the river of the pass is similar to the real bridge, but the "deep gorge" and the "steel" bridge are utterly unlike the Puente de la Cantina.

In the late fifties Hemingway told Spanish novelist José Luis Castillo-Puche a number of times that he would take him to "the bridge" but he apparently never did, and Castillo-Puche concluded that the bridge in the novel "had never existed," that it had been "a figment of his imagination: he had first constructed it and then destroyed it, entirely in his mind." Furthermore, such an invention "didn't lessen the value of the novel at all; in a certain sense it might even enhance it." He goes on to ruminate that no real bridge could have had the importance given to the one in the novel and to note that "there had been no guerrilla forces, either large or small isolated bands, operating in this sector during the war."[6]

Did Hemingway simply invent it all out of thin air? What bothers Castillo-Puche most is something that has bothered many of the Spanish critics of the book, as we have noted: "And might not the fact that the bridge episode was a historical distortion detract somewhat from the otherwise admirable realism of the book?" (Castillo-Puche,

Hemingway at the "bridge site," that is, the stone bridge known as the Puente de la Cantina or the Puente del Penon. This photograph, probably by Mary Hemingway in 1954, shows the approximate place where Hemingway had envisioned his bridge, but the bridge in the photo is clearly not a steel bridge over a gorge, which Hemingway had invented.

Courtesy of the Hemingway Collection, John F. Kennedy Library. (Photo no. EH7400P)

310). It troubles Castillo-Puche that Hemingway kept telling him about the bridge as if it existed. He admits that "What an author invents often becomes part of himself," but he cannot quite accept Hemingway's vivid descriptions of something so apparently imaginary (Castillo-Puche, 311).

Hemingway had a very explicit idea of his bridge in mind at the time of publication of the novel. When he received a tentative dust jacket showing, ironically perhaps from our point of view, a *stone* bridge, he wrote to Charles Scribner, saying the jacket "seems o.k. although I know nothing about them. Except that the bridge should be a thin high arching metal, cantilever bridge instead of a stone bridge. It will go in there o.k. Should be high, thin and spidery looking. Blowing up that stone bridge in the picture wouldn't hold up anything. If bridge is used it must look to be distant and to be bridgeing a steep gorge" (*Letters*, 508).

It is pretty clear from that letter that Hemingway was making it all up, as we had suspected, and inventing it all without the least thought to Castillo-Puche's idea of distortion. But, the question remains, what was he making it up from? Was it pure imagination, so to speak, or something concrete—or should I say metal?

Peter Wyden has supplied one interesting answer. He uses a quote from the novel as his epigraph: "Robert Jordan lay behind the trunk of a pine tree on the slope of the hill above the road and the bridge and watched it become daylight. . . . Below he saw, through the light mist that rose from the stream bed, the steel of the bridge, straight and rigid across the gap . . . spidery and fine. . . . "[7] Wyden goes on to tell the story of the battle at the Arganda Bridge over the Jarama River, some twenty kilometers southeast of Madrid on the all-important Valencia road that linked the temporary capital of the Republic in Valencia with Madrid. The bridge, a long, narrow, metal suspension bridge, was the key to the road and the road was Madrid's "lifeline." It was defended bravely, even heroically, by French volunteers of the XII International Brigade in February 1937.

Hemingway arrived in Spain shortly after that, and hearing of the gallant stand, wanted to incorporate the Arganda bridge into the film *The Spanish Earth*. Gustav Regler was commissar—communist political officer—for the XII Brigade, and being a lapsed German Catholic and a none-too-enchanted communist, he and Hemingway quickly became friends. It was Regler who first told Hemingway about André Marty and "how Marty had wanted to shoot the Arganda wine-looters," the remnants of the French troops who had defended the bridge (Wyden, 303). Hemingway was outraged, for the few surviving men had simply "liberated" an abandoned wine cellar, and he would have the final word on Marty in *For Whom the Bell Tolls*. Hemingway got along famously with the French survivors, was very moved by their heroism, loved the XII Brigade, and came to hate Marty. Wyden, perhaps overdoing the drama, reports that " . . . when Regler confided . . . such outrages to him during their later encounters, Ernest was reduced to tears" (Wyden, 303).

Most of all, for our purposes, Wyden believes that "The Arganda Bridge would stay with Hemingway and his readers forever. It became the model for the bridge that Ernest's hero, Robert Jordan, was assigned to blow up in *For Whom the Bell Tolls*" (Wyden, 303). Perhaps, but I am more inclined to believe that Hemingway invented it from some other source. William Braasch Watson, historian of the Spanish Civil War, believes Hemingway may have taken his structure from the *Engineer Field Manual* (a source we will examine further in chapter twelve), "where a number of truss-structured bridges are illustrated and the manner of placing explosives in those truss sections is explained and illustrated."[8] Watson's theory seems more credible since the low Arganda bridge—good as Wyden's story is—is certainly not "high, thin and spidery looking," as Hemingway had described it.

Castillo-Puche, still worrying about the bridge, writes, "As time went by I became more and more convinced that *For Whom the Bell Tolls* contained a number of errors . . . but I no longer questioned people to try to ascertain the real facts. Would the precise truth have made Ernest's story any more valuable as a human document and work of literature?" The trees here seem clearly in danger of blocking the view of the forest. By refusing to abandon his literal stance, our Spanish critic runs the risk of failing to understand the novel's higher purpose. He almost struggles free: "The real impact of his book, its magnificent powers of revelation belonged to a much higher order of truth." Yes.

La Curva del Monje (the Monk's Cave) is not a cave at all but a slab of granite that suggests the entrance to a cave. There are no caves in this area. Pablo's refuge was another of Hemingway's inventions.

Photograph by the author.

The Arganda Bridge over the Jarama River southeast of Madrid. Was this the kind of structure Hemingway had in mind? He was certainly well acquainted with this bridge, and it is closer to the descriptions in the novel than the stone bridge in the Guadarrama Mountains. Still, this bridge is quite low. Most probably the high "spidery" bridge itself was a creation of Hemingway, possibly inspired by the *Engineer Field Manual*.

Photograph by the author.

But what is that order? "To my mind, the most important thing was Ernesto's noble idealism, which had been strikingly evident throughout the struggle, and equally evident twenty years after the war had ended" (Castillo-Puche, 310).

If Castillo-Puche is right, we should read the novel because Hemingway is a nice, that is to say, noble, guy—something, by the way, not very many people have seriously accused him of. Isn't it more enlightening to think the higher order of truth is the art of the storyteller? That for his setting, sometimes more Homeric than historic, he deepened a mountain stream into a gorge? That he saw in the suggestion of a cave's mouth a depth in the Spanish earth sufficient to hide his fugitive band? That he turned a stone bridge into "the steel of the bridge, straight and rigid across the gap" and at the same time something "spidery and fine in the mist that hung over the stream" (431), something that if blown properly could help stop the march of fascism forever?

9

The Characters: Instead of Just a Hero

In 1932 Hemingway wrote to John Dos Passos, praising his novel *1919*, the second volume of the *U.S.A.* trilogy. He counseled the following: "Now watch one thing. In the 3rd volume don't let yourself slip and get any perfect characters in. . . . If you get a noble communist remember the bastard probably masturbates and is jallous as a cat. Keep them people, people, people, and don't let them get to be symbols" (*Letters*, 354). In writing *For Whom the Bell Tolls* Hemingway would take his own advice almost right down to the habits of the noble communist, as we shall see.

We have already examined the setting of the novel as circular. Yet the circularity of the setting, and even of the plot, comes from the characters, especially Robert Jordan. As Hemingway was agonizing over the ending (including considering an epilogue), he wrote to Perkins, "But it really stops where Jordan is feeling his heart beating against the pine needle floor of the forest," completing the circle (without the unneeded epilogue). As he explained to Perkins:

> You see every damned word and action in this book depends on every other word and action. You see he's laying there on the pine needles at the start and that is where he is at the end. He has had

his problem and all his life before him at the start and he has all
his life in those days and, at the end there is only death there for
him and he truly isn't afraid of it at all because he has a chance to
finish his mission. (*Letters*, 514)

Setting, plot, and character all function within the same circle, what
Carlos Baker has called "the great wheel" (Baker 1972, 259-63).

Yet there is another circular way to see the characters in *For
Whom the Bell Tolls*. Baker suggested that as well: "In fact
Hemingway's novel follows an architectural plan comparable to that
of a Spanish bullring, which is constructed in a series of concentric circles, so arranged that from any point one can watch the action taking
place at the center" (Baker 1972, 260). Angel Capellán, following
Baker's lead, has constructed the actual concentric diagram with the
cave and the bridge in the center, the nearby towns in the next circle,
beyond that Madrid and other Spanish cities, then European countries,
and finally in the last circle, the U.S.A. (Capellán, 252).

All the above makes good sense, but I want us to look at a different set of circles that only involve the characters themselves. My circles
are concentric too, and there are three of them. In the outer circle are
real people, actual historical characters. In the middle circle are real
but disguised people. In the inner circle are invented people—invented from experience and reality sometimes, but invented, nonetheless.
And at the epicenter (a deliberately seismological term because of its
significance in the discussion of love to follow) are Robert and María.

The circles are not always perfectly concentric and they are not
always separate. Robert Jordan's memories of Gaylord's in Madrid,
for example, show how these circles fade into each other with characters from all three circles present there. All these fluid circles really do
is show us distance and proximity or historicity and invention. The
distant outer circles provide objectivity, credibility, and veracity for the
invented central drama. There is a real, verifiable, historical war going
on around the invented central action.

If we think of the characters like the cast of a play, the main
characters, who play close downstage, are invented. Farther upstage

are the disguised characters—General Golz, for example—who interact with the main characters, occasionally coming downstage—
Karkov, for example, talking to Jordan at Gaylord's in chapter
eighteen—and becoming part of the center of our attention. Far
upstage, although spotlighted at times, are the historical characters,
such as André Marty. Some are even off the stage altogether and are
only mentioned by the others, such as La Pasionaria.

The point, however, is not the structure itself, but the fact that
Hemingway was consciously working with, and causing to interact,
real people, disguised real people, and invented characters. The real-
ness of the real people although they now may seem obscure, gives
the novel a wonderful sense of verisimilitude; and the heightened
reality of the invented characters—more real than real, truer than
true—helps create the mythic dimension of the novel. The mythic
dimension that arises from invention is indeed one of the main attrac-
tions of fiction.

Hemingway's invented novel is, in that sense, vastly superior to
his own reality-based stories about the war. He always carefully tem-
pers the mythic or romantic elements with the real, keeping his people
people and never letting them become symbols. In this context it is
perhaps easier to understand what Robert A. Martin means by the
"masterful blend of fact and fiction" and how, through that blend,
"*For Whom the Bell Tolls* achieves the status of a classic war novel"
(Martin, 219).

It would be tedious to examine the backgrounds of every single
one of the real people mentioned in or appearing in *For Whom the Bell
Tolls*, so we will look at a few representatives. We need to remember
that it is the depiction of some of these real people that has caused
much negative criticism of the novel, particularly of the leftist political
variety.

Dolores Ibarruri Gómez, known as La Pasionaria, was the leg-
endary orator whose dictum, *"No pasarán,"* (They shall not pass [enter
into or through Madrid]) became the rallying cry for the defense of
Madrid in the first days of the war and eventually the battle cry of
Republican Spain. Hemingway himself did not like La Pasionaria

much: "Dolores always made me vomit always," he reportedly told friends (Baker 1969, 347). As Baker points out, "For all his Loyalist sympathies, he had never been able to swallow the program of propaganda which had elevated Dolores Ibarruri, a Communist peasant woman from the Basque provinces, into La Pasionaria (The Passion Flower), a kind of leftist saint" (Baker 1969, 347).

Hemingway used the figure of Ibarruri twice for ironic effect. In chapter twenty-seven, El Sordo's last stand, the young communist partizan Joaquín begins to quote communist slogans to bolster, he thinks, his own and the others' morale:

> "*Resistir y fortificar es vencer,*" Joaquín said, his mouth stiff with the dryness of fear which surpassed the normal thirst of battle. It was one of the slogans of the Communist party and it meant "Hold out and fortify, and you will win." (308)

The other men make fun of him, of course, but Joaquín, so far undaunted, quotes La Pasionaria: "Pasionaria says it is better to die on your feet than to live on your knees" (309). Again the other men scorn what he says and one remarks: "If thou believest so much in thy Pasionaria, get her to get us off this hill" (309).

This not so comic banter leads up to their slaughter, and we see what Hemingway has prepared for us as the planes bomb the remnants of the band into oblivion:

> "Pasionaria says 'Better to die on thy—'" Joaquín was saying to himself as the drone came nearer them. Then he shifted suddenly into "Hail Mary, full of grace, the Lord is with thee. . . . " (321)

Finishing the "Hail Mary," he begins an act of contrition as the planes close in; forgetting that, "All he could remember was at the hour of our death. Amen. At the hour of our death. Amen. At the hour. At the hour. At the hour. Amen. The others were all firing. Now and at the hour of our death. Amen" (321). It is one of the most brilliantly pathetic moments in Hemingway's writing, the boy abandoning the useless slogans, reverting to the only salvation he knows as the bombs explode and the earth moves, not in ecstatic love but at the hour of their death.

The other instance occurs in chapter thirty-two, in Madrid the night before the attack is to begin. The puffy-eyed correspondent for the Soviet newspaper *Izvestia* (probably based on the real correspondent Ilya Ehrenburg, whom Hemingway knew) tells the Russian journalist Karkov that "the fascists have been fighting among themselves near Segovia. They have been forced to quell the mutinies with automatic rifle and machine gun fire. In the afternoon they were bombing their own troops with planes" (357). We never find out positively whether this report is feeble-mindedly wrong or intentionally distorted, although the general stupidity and laxness prevalent in this scene suggest the former. We do, however, find out the puffy-eyed man's source:

> "Dolores brought the news herself. She was here with the news and was in such a state of radiant exultation as I have never seen. The truth of the news shone from her face. That great face—" he said happily. (357)

It is the puffy-eyed man as much as Ibarruri whom Hemingway is pursuing in this passage. A nameless sympathetic Hungarian general, based clearly on Hemingway's good friend General "Lukács," merely reports that she said, "Something about the fascists fighting among themselves. Beautiful if true" (358). What makes her report absurd, and the puffy-eyed man's account of her report the ultimate absurdity—all of this invented by Hemingway—is that what they are reporting is the destruction of El Sordo's band. These ironic scenes made the Left furious, but they linked the bands in the mountains to the real war and its real waging from inside Madrid. They also made clear Hemingway's feelings—through Jordan when necessary, but here straight from the omniscient narrator—about the stupidity, the ineptitude, and the hypocrisy that were rampant among some of the communists.

The case Hemingway made against Marty—the real André Marty, the chief commissar, which is to say the high communist polit-

From left to right: Ilya Ehrenburg, Ernest Hemingway, and Gustav Regler. Ehrenburg was the correspondent for the Soviet newspaper *Izvestia*. Gustav Regler, who became a close friend of Hemingway, was the commissar—the communist political officer—of the XII International Brigade. This photo was taken in spring 1937.

Courtesy of the Hemingway Collection, John F. Kennedy Library. (Photo no. EH5449

ical official in charge of the International Brigades—is even stronger. Marty, a real person in a fictional situation, becomes one of the true villains of the novel. Unlike La Pasionaria, who is only condemned for her rhetoric, Marty deliberately holds up Robert Jordan's message, thereby causing the attack to take place in spite of the warning Jordan has sent. He is not the sole villain, to be sure: "It is doubtful if the outcome of Andrés's mission would have been any different if he and Gomez had been allowed to proceed without André Marty's hindrance" (423). But Hemingway's portrait of him as an insane fool is definitive, an insane fool unfortunately in charge, about whom General Golz thinks, "Damn you to hell for all the men you've killed by interfering in matters you know nothing of" (423).

Hemingway was justified in his portrayal of Marty, no matter how much it infuriated the Left. But what probably irritated them most was not a more or less accurate picture of Marty—Hugh Thomas writes that his Stalinist-purging paranoia was real enough: "Only Stalin himself had a more suspicious nature than André Marty" (Thomas, 458)—but the fact that Hemingway invented this episode to indict Marty as one of the arch-villains in the Spanish Civil War.

So it must have seemed to them at any rate, but as Jeffrey Meyers has pointed out, Hemingway may have loosely based the Marty scenes on an actual incident that occurred on the Córdoba front earlier in the war.[1] As we already have seen, Hemingway had heard of and hated Marty since his first days at the Arganda bridge in early 1937, when his friend Gustav Regler had informed him of Marty's suspicions and atrocities. In *For Whom the Bell Tolls* Hemingway was able to get revenge and turn it into superb narrative strategy.

Jeffrey Meyers has an interesting theory which centers in part on this fictional use of Marty. He believes that *For Whom the Bell Tolls* is "an allegory of, as well as an explanation of, the Loyalist defeat in the Spanish war." I need to cite Meyer's careful wording in full to make his point clear:

> Andrés's journey through enemy lines—he is "impeded by the ignorance of the anarchists. Then by the sloth of a bureaucratic fascist. Now by thy oversuspicion of a Communist" (420)—is

FOR WHOM THE BELL TOLLS

obstructed by the factionalism of the Left and by the dominance
of political commissars over military commanders, and symbolizes
the *betrayal* of Spain by the *foreigners*. Andrés's inability to convince his allies to call off the attack represents the Loyalists' failure to persuade France and England to stop the German and
Italian invasion. Hemingway's allegory explains the three main
reasons for the Loyalist defeat: the *factionalism* of the Left, the
interference (at the time of the Russian Purge Trials) of political
commissars, and the successful intervention of Hitler's and
Mussolini's armies while the democratic countries remained passive and indifferent. (Meyers 1988, 16; my emphasis)

Even if we do not subscribe wholeheartedly to Meyers's idea of allegory, calling the impediments to Andrés's mission perhaps representa-
tions instead of anything so abstracted as allegory—even so, Meyers's
points about why the Republic lost, and Hemingway's careful and
intentional inclusion of a representation of each one, should not be
lost on us.

Meyers goes on to condemn—correctly—Kenneth Lynn's recent
biography for its "sneers at Hemingway's 'lack of political sophistica-
tion' and 'service for Stalin'" which "blindly ignores the fact that
Hemingway was more critical of the Communists than almost anyone
else of the Left" (Meyers 1988, 16). Meyers concludes that
Hemingway's "fictional rather than propagandistic account of the
Communist role in the war did not advance the cause of the
Revolution," but that his "insight about the complexity of the Spanish
tragedy, written immediately after the events it records, makes *For
Whom the Bell Tolls* the greatest political novel in American literature"
(Meyers 1988, 16-17).

To the extent that Meyers is correct, the greatness of the novel
depends in no small way on the criticism of real people, including such
Republican commanders as Lister, Modesto, and Valentín González
(called El Campesino) about whom Hemingway had been very compli-
mentary in the propaganda film *The Spanish Earth*. A large measure of
the greatness of the novel also comes from the fictional manipulation
of real people such as Marty. Hemingway was undoubtedly aware that

his manipulated portrait of Marty, immortalized in fiction, far surpassed any vengeance he could have wreaked on Marty in "real life."

Not all the "real" people are portrayed negatively in *For Whom the Bell Tolls*. Consider, for example, the case of General Gustavo Durán. Unlike generals Modesto, Lister, and El Campesino, all of whom were workers and communists, Gustavo Durán was a cultured, upper class, talented musician. Durán later became a close enough friend for Hemingway to ask him to read the galleys of *For Whom the Bell Tolls*, ostensibly to check the Spanish for errors (see Appendix).

Robert Jordan remembers Durán fondly and thinks of him as a fine example:

> Just remember Durán, who never had any military training and who was a composer and lad about town before the movement and is now a damned good general commanding a brigade. It was all as simple and easy to learn and understand to Durán as chess to a child chess prodigy. . . . Old Durán. It would be good to see Durán again. (335)

These were indeed lofty words for a man whom Hemingway praised, as Jeffrey Meyers phrases it, "as no other contemporary was ever praised by Hemingway" (Meyers 1988, 10). Hemingway was even more extravagant about Durán after the war, calling him his "God damn hero," until their relationship soured a few years later in Cuba (Baker 1969, 350 and 378-79).

Two other real characters, one mentioned by name and the other not, are worth looking at briefly. Robert Jordan tells María that when they go to Madrid they can have a servant: "I can get Petra who is at the hotel [Florida] if she pleases thee. She cooks well and is clean. I have eaten there with newspapermen that she cooks for. They have electric stoves in their rooms" (347). Petra was also a character in Hemingway's play *The Fifth Column*; that is, she was both the chambermaid for Philip Rawlings at the Hotel Florida in the play and for Ernest Hemingway in reality. In the play Petra was also Dorothy's confidante, and now in *For Whom the Bell Tolls* she would apparently be suitable to work for María.

The newspapermen with electric stoves in their rooms are also interesting since Hemingway himself, who had special access to scarce food supplies and gasoline that other correspondents did not have, was the one best known for the "delicious odors of percolating coffee and frying ham" occasionally emanating from his Hotel Florida room (Baker 1969, 305). The newspapermen Robert Jordan ate with, then, were undoubtedly men such as Sefton Delmer of the London *Daily Mail*, Herbert Matthews of the *New York Times*—two skilled professional journalists already living at the Hotel Florida when Hemingway arrived—and Hemingway himself, NANA correspondent, possibly appearing in an unidentified, almost Hitchcockesque vignette. The scene serves little purpose in the novel except as inside humor to draw our attention to how these circles of reality and invention blend together at a point where Robert Jordan and Ernest Hemingway, character and author, may even share a meal.

Two important characters who are real people appear with fictive names. One is the *Pravda* correspondent Karkov, whose real name was Mikhail Koltsov; and the other is General Golz, whose real name in Polish, as I mentioned earlier, was Karol Swierczewski but whose *nom de guerre* in Spain was "General Walter." General Walter was in reality in charge of the failed La Granja offensive. Both characters—both men—were admired and respected by Hemingway and consequently by Robert Jordan.

Hemingway often saw Koltsov at the Russian headquarters in the Hotel Gaylord and the extensive Gaylord's chapter (eighteen) is based closely on Hemingway's own experiences there with the Russians. It is important to remember that Koltsov was a personal agent for Stalin; Robert Jordan remembers that Karkov was "in direct communication with Stalin" and "was at this moment one of the three most important men in Spain" (424). Hemingway liked Koltsov and Robert Jordan likes Karkov: "He had liked Karkov. . . . Karkov was the most intelligent man he had ever met. . . . he had more brains and more inner dignity and outer insolence and humor than any man he had ever known" (231).

Years later Hemingway would sing Koltsov's praises to his friend Bernard Berenson in a letter we have already examined in a political context: "He knew I was not a Communist and never would be one. But because he believed in me as a writer he tried to show me how everything was run so that I could give a true account of it" (*Letters*, 789). As Peter Wyden has grandly remarked, "At the Gaylord, Koltzov created a salon that became Hemingway's university" (Wyden, 328).

By the same token Karkov explains many things to Jordan about the Russians, the communists, the Stalinist purges, the anarchists, and so forth. Chapter eighteen is, in fact, a veritable treasure trove of insider information, containing virtually everything that Hemingway had learned as a correspondent that had any relevance to the events in the novel. Spanish Civil War historian Hugh Thomas calls chapter eighteen "brilliant" (Thomas, 394, n. 1).

Karkov treats Robert Jordan much the same as Koltsov had treated Hemingway: "I think you write absolutely truly and that is very rare. So I would like you to know some things" (248). What Hemingway learned through Koltsov becomes what Jordan learns from Karkov, and the resulting sense of reality, of what was really happening, was one of Hemingway's finest achievements in the novel.

Even though some of the details may not seem to have the relevance today that they had at the time of the novel's publication, this outer ring of historical truth and accuracy—virtually every one of Hemingway's evaluations has stood the test of time—gives the novel another significant measure of its greatness. To study this aspect in detail is to quiet forever the critics who whined about Hemingway's political ingenuousness.

After talking with Karkov, Jordan thinks, "He would write a book when he got through with this. But only about the things he knew, truly . . . " (248). This is Hemingway's way of alerting the reader that the political information about this most complex of conflicts was also the truest account that he, Hemingway, could write. As Robert Jordan realizes, "The things he had come to know in this war were not so simple" (248).

General Golz is also a sympathetic character. Hemingway got to know the real General Walter in the battle for the defense of Madrid and was impressed by his military capability and by his unusual appearance. Robert Jordan remembers his fictional counterpart " . . .

with his strange white face that never tanned, his hawk eyes, the big nose and thin lips and the shaven head crossed with wrinkles and with scars" (8).

One of General Walter's best traits was his ability to joke regardless of the circumstances. Hemingway praised his grace under pressure in a letter to the critic Edmund Wilson: "I saw Walter at a bridge with nothing to blow it and the fascists tanks on the other side thinking it was mined and four of us watching them. Under these circumstances Walter could make jokes" (*Letters*, 794).

In a letter to his friend Evan Shipman, he recounted an anecdote involving the French novelist André Malraux and General Walter: "Am always reminded of the time in Spain when Malraux asked Walter what he thought on some subject and Walter said 'Pense? Moi pense pas. Moi general sovietique. Pense jamais. [Think? Me/I never think. Me/I soviet general. Never think.]'" (*Letters*, 538).

Evidently Hemingway found this so amusing and characteristic of General Walter that he has Golz tell Robert Jordan: "You never think about only girls. I never think at all. Why should I? I am *Général Sovietique*. I never think. Do not try to trap me into thinking" (8). This clever bit of dialogue not only characterizes Golz, it also sets up the girl about to enter the picture and introduces, comically, the need to avoid thinking that Jordan will voice throughout the novel. As he remarks later to Karkov, "My mind is in suspension until we win the war" (245).

It is important to remember that the challenge to André Marty's insane authority and the condemnation of Marty come precisely from these two characters, Karkov and General Golz, in chapter forty-two. Perhaps because these incidents were fictional, Hemingway decided to change their names. He was concerned about potential liability and possibly about political consequences. We know this since, regarding Marty, whose name he decidedly did not want to change, he wrote to Charles Scribner, "One other thing—Andre Marty is the name of a real person. He has fled from France to Russia under sentence of death. . . . He could never come to U.S. under any circumstances. He cannot go back to France unless the Communists come into power. Can he sue?" (*Letters*, 509).

The Characters: Instead of Just a Hero

Golz is called Golz—actually he first spells it "Goltz"—from the beginning of the earliest manuscript (KL/EH, item 83, p. 4), so Hemingway obviously intended the name change from the novel's inception. Something Hemingway evidently told his Polish translator, Bronislaw Zielinski, and which Zielinski wrote to Jeffrey Meyers, may provide Hemingway's deeper motive for the name changes of General Walter and by extension of Koltsov. Zielinski apparently asked Hemingway why, when so many appeared under their own names, he had used neither Walter nor Swierczewski, to which Hemingway replied: "He was such a splendid man and splendid soldier that I wouldn't dare to present him in *fictitious* situations, and put in his mouth *fictitious* words" (Meyers 1988, 13; my emphasis). The fact that Hemingway does, in fact, also mention General Walter by name in the novel, but in a historical context, may bear this statement out. Karkov tells Jordan that the anarchists "made one plot you know to kill me, to kill Walter, to kill Modesto, and to kill Prieto" (247), all of whose names were real, except, of course, the speaker's.

At any event General Golz has the last word when he thinks ironically, having gotten Jordan's message too late, "No. *Rien à faire. Rien. Faut pas penser. Faut accepter* [Nothing to do. Nothing. No need to think. Need to accept]" (429). Whatever his motive for the name changes, these disguised and "fictitious" real people served Hemingway's purposes perfectly by exposing the betrayal of the offensive and, by extension, of the Republic.

The most important *invented* character in the novel, aside from Robert Jordan and María, the one that occupies most of our attention and no little speculation on the part of critics as to the sources for her invention, is Pilar. Jeffrey Meyers, in his biography of Hemingway, wrote that "Pilar, the domineering, operatic leader of the guerrilla group, has more than a touch of Grace Hemingway's forceful personality."[2] I disagree and do not find Pilar particularly "operatic," nor in any way like Hemingway's midwestern, Protestant mother, whom he did not particularly like. Hemingway unequivocally loves, admires, and respects his character Pilar, who is named for the Patroness of Spain, Nuestra Señora del Pilar, for whom he had earlier named his prized fishing boat and for whom he intended to name a daughter, if he ever had one.

Nor can I agree with Joseph Waldmeir that "when he created Pilar, he was thinking primarily of Gertrude Stein."[3] Waldmeir bases this view on Stein's size, her lesbianism, and a passage about Stein herself in the novel. Stein and Pilar are roughly the same size but so was Hemingway's mother and the singer Kate Smith, who will also enter the picture before too long.

Pilar is clearly not a lesbian as she states, as María states, and as Jordan states (155, 154, 173). As Jordan realizes, Pilar's attraction to María was vicarious, "But it wasn't evil. It was only wanting to keep her hold on life. To keep it *through* Maria" (176, my emphasis).

The passage Waldmeir offers as example has nothing to do with Pilar. Agustín and Robert Jordan are discussing onions as a breakfast food and Agustín says that, aside from the odor, onions are like roses. And Jordan starts the word play: "A rose is a rose is an onion," he begins, parodying Stein's famous dictum "A rose is a rose is a rose." Then taking it further:

> "An onion is an onion is an onion," Robert Jordan said cheerily and, he thought, a stone is a stein is a rock is a boulder is a pebble. (289)

Nice word play, only possible in English, for our ears only (i.e., not Agustín's), a definite reference to Gertrude Stein—making her a pebble, and a nonsensical one at that—but in no way is the passage connected to Pilar. Waldmeir opines that Hemingway is "making sure that via the onion-rose-Stein-stone (and by logical extension, Pilar) puns that the reader . . . gets the similarities between Gertrude and Pilar which he may have only suspected before" (Waldmeir, 45).

Unfortunately for Waldmeir's theory, though, precisely the opposite is true. Stein ends as pebble while Pilar has a name which connotes exactly the reverse: support, bastion, stone post, milestone, pillar, basin, bowl, Patroness of Spain, Spanishness itself. Nuestra Señora del Pilar's day is the twelfth of October, *día de la Hispanidad*, day of Hispanicity, if you will, our Columbus Day. And her *pilar*, her

pillar, is a sacred column of marble worn away by the kiss of count-
less generations of worshipers. Tradition has it that on 2 January, in
the year 40 A.D., the Virgin appeared miraculously to St. James,
known in Spanish as Santiago (who is, not coincidentally, the Patron
of Spain), leaving her *pilar*, her pillar, as proof of her apparition, the
extremely early date of which makes it the earliest Marian sanctuary
in Spain.

Clearly, I think we can conclude that it was not Gertrude Stein
whom Hemingway had in mind, anymore than it was La Pasionaria
upon "whose physical appearance, whose convictions, whose voice
and whose very gestures" Pilar was based, as Alvah Bessie attempted to
maintain (Bessie, 14). In fact, it was no family member, no literary
type, certainly no foreigner, and no political figure from whom she
was created.

I would much rather agree with John J. Teunissen that Pilar—
part Gypsy and something of a seer, with her "heavy brown face with
the high Indian cheekbones (298)"; whose bed "smelt the way an
Indian's bed does (360)"—is a primitive, something of an animist, and
something of a shaman, "the Wise Old Woman" who can use icon and
archetype "in leading the way back and down to the dark gods within
the individual and group psyche."[4] But we must remember that within
that shamanistic characterization, she is also quintessentially Spanish,
hence her very important and characteristic name, Pilar.

Edward F. Stanton has understood the complex figure of Pilar
well, describing her, not unjustifiably, as "the most complex character
in all of Hemingway's fiction." Stanton calls her "a kind of witch or
shaman who possesses an ancient, secret knowledge of the world,"
whose "wisdom is older than science," who is "an earth mother," and
who has a "secret knowledge of the subconscious and of death." He
connects Pilar to the Spanish concept of *duende*, which he defines in
the words of the great Spanish poet Federico García Lorca as "the spirit of the earth." He concludes that "she is the main presence of the
novel, in many ways even more important than Robert Jordan," that
she personifies "the night mind and a new feminine consciousness [in]
Hemingway's work," and finally that "She is Spain, the Spanish
earth."[5]

Stanton's views on Pilar summarize quite well what I believe Hemingway was attempting with her character. Stanton gets to the essence of Pilar, who is in turn the essence of Spain, the "dark wisdom" which "stretches back in time long before the discovery of Jordan's America" (Stanton, 172).

Contrary to the theories about Grace Hemingway and Gertrude Stein and La Pasionaria, we have Hemingway's actual statements about Pilar's origins. In a letter to Charles Scribner, in which Hemingway justified the famous "smell of death" passage, he also told Scribner what he left out: "I haven't just put every goddamned thing I know or ever heard in. I didn't put in *Pilar's husband* (really Rafael el Gallo) being impotent on his wedding night . . . " (*Letters*, 508; my emphasis).

Rafael Gómez Ortega, the great artist of the bullring known as El Gallo, was from the most famous Spanish Gypsy clan of all time. For seven or eight generations, going back at least as far as 1800, from Cádiz and Sevilla, they dominated flamenco music and toreo. Noted flamencologist D. E. Pohren calls the Ortegas (Rafael's mother's side) "The most illustrious bullfight and flamenco family of all time."[6]

In early 1911—Hemingway would have been eleven at the time, so he obviously heard about it—Rafael el Gallo married Pastora Imperio, whose real name was Pastora Rojas Monje. Born in Sevilla in 1889, she was the daughter of the famous nineteenth-century Gypsy dancer *La mejorana*. Pastora Imperio was Pilar.

Stanton knew this because he read an unpublished Hemingway letter at the Kennedy Library in which Hemingway said, "I know it is not like Carmen anymore than Pastora Imperio (Pilar) is like Kate Smith" (Stanton, 170; the reference to Pilar in parentheses is Hemingway's; "it" means the novel and "Carmen" means the opera; the singer Kate Smith—like Gertrude Stein, Grace Hemingway, and Pilar—was a large woman). So there is no doubt that he based Pilar on Pastora Imperio. In fact, the only question remaining is to what extent, and that is where Stanton and I disagree. He maintains that "Hemingway created her character from his own imagination, but he based her *in part* on Pastora Imperio because Pilar has the ineffable power of duende associated with the famous singer" (Stanton, 171; my emphasis).

The Characters: Instead of Just a Hero

Of course he created her from his imagination. As Hemingway's most autobiographical character, the young writer Nick Adams, muses, "Nick in the stories was never himself. He made him up."[7] That is, thinks Nick, Nick made *himself up* in the stories. In other words he used a real person, himself, but imagined the action and imagined himself as the character. That is one of the most important and most characteristic devices Hemingway used in his fiction. It is one of the reasons his fiction seems so real. Pilar works so well and is so complex because she truly is Pastora. As Hemingway said of *The Sun Also Rises*, "I took real people in that one and I controlled what they did. I made it all up" (*Letters*, 400).

In *Death in the Afternoon* he remarked, "When writing a novel a writer should create living people; people not characters. . . . People in a novel, not skillfully constructed *characters*, must be projected from the writer's assimilated experience, from his knowledge, from his head, from his heart and from all there is of him. If he ever has luck as well as seriousness and gets them out entire they will have more than one dimension and they will last a long time" (*DIA*, 191). With Pilar he had luck and seriousness: she is entire, has many dimensions, and will last a long time, precisely because he had the perfect person, Pastora Imperio, to invent her from.

Stanton recalls that Pastora was described by Hemingway in an unpublished passage from *Death in the Afternoon* as one of the "hard-voiced singers" (Stanton, 170), but the quotation of only that phrase does not do justice to her nor to what Hemingway meant. And he calls her a singer when in reality she was primarily a dancer, but also a singer, a reciter, and an actress. Pastora was well known for her long repertory and particularly for her "arm dance"—*baile de brazos*—and for her spontaneous, unchoreographed dances. Hemingway described her in that cut passage as "immense," referring to her size and her artistic stature. He describes the fading beauty of some of the then current female flamenco performers but remarks that Pastora was "the only one that lasts forever" and laments not having seen her when she was young because he has been told that he cannot now "realize what she was."[8]

D. E. Pohren described Pastora in 1963 as "universally considered the finest remaining interpreter of the old school of feminine dance" (Pohren, 220). Manuel de Falla's *El amor brujo* was written expressly for Pastora. Pohren relates how

> Pastora remembers nostalgically when she and Ramón [Montoya] would step out alone on the stage, he to "spin a silver *soleá*" on his guitar, she to "weave an emotional web," creating, improvising, until the entire house was on its feet roaring its approval. . . . Every old *aficionado* who saw Pastora verifies her story, and then adds great eulogies of his own. (Pohren, 222)

During the twenties—when Hemingway was often in Madrid—she played constantly at the Teatro Romea, the Madrid Cinema, the Teatro Maravillas and the Teatro de la Latina. The poet Ramón Díaz Mirete summed her up as "¡Andalucía!" And novelist Tomás Borrás wrote, "*Pastora Imperio es la pasión de una raza* (Pastora Imperio is the [incarnation of the] passion of a race [i.e., the Spanish people]).[9] Pastora, born ten years before Hemingway, lived until 1979. She did have, as Stanton claimed, "the ineffable power of duende," the spirit of the Spanish earth, and Hemingway's choice to use her as a model—not "in part" but all of her, "immense"—for his imagined Pilar was a stroke of genius.

All the characters are not traceable to such models as Pastora, but we do know something about the origins of María. Carlos Baker, as usual, was the first to bring it to our attention, using information he got from Abraham Lincoln Brigade veteran Fred Keller:

> But the most memorable result of Ernest's visit to Mataró was his meeting with one of the nurses, a quiet and devoted Spanish girl named María, who struck all her charges as the very "soul of serenity." Early in the war she had been raped by Fascist soldiers. (Baker 1969, 328)

Peter Wyden interviewed Fred Keller later on and got more details:

The Characters: Instead of Just a Hero

> Then Fred told Ernest they should all do something special for two young Spanish *sanitarias*, the two nurse's aides who had been taking care of him. The prettier one was María: shy, serene, about 24. She was a Communist, like her father, who had been executed in Andalusia when the war broke out. María had been imprisoned and, over the months, raped 24 times.
>
> The correspondents got local fishermen to dig a hole in the Mataró beach and fry a feast of freshly caught pompano that night. Hemingway met María and remembered. (Wyden, 468)

This description of María sounds a bit too perfect to be altogether believable, but unless Keller made the whole story up, it probably represents a certain embellished truth.

Baker added another aspect to María, observing that her "physical characteristics, including the blond hair 'like a wheatfield in the wind,' were evidently designed as a secret tribute to Martha Gellhorn" (Baker 1969, 348). Baker told Stanton he thought María was "part M. Gellhorn (1/4) and the rest imagination" (Stanton, 173). Surely the fictional María was a mixture of the Andalusian nurse's aide, Martha Gellhorn, and imagination. The attributes Hemingway drew from the nurse's aide María are obvious enough: the executed father, the rapes, her name. Notice, however, that although she and Pastora are Andalusians, Hemingway, who had an odd bias against the south of Spain until his later trips in the fifties, turns them as characters into Castilians and changes María's family's politics into support for the Republic.

Much of the physical aspect of the fictional María does undoubtedly come from Martha Gellhorn, and the tribute is not really secret at all. María's coloring, her hair, and her long legs are certainly reminiscent of Martha Gellhorn. María's nickname also comes from the same source. Stanton writes that two unpublished fragments in the Kennedy Library "suggest quite strongly that 'Rabbit' was a nickname used by EH for Martha Gellhorn" (Stanton, 229).

Actually Stanton is understating the case: in both fragments the man is very obviously the Hemingway-like character from the Civil War short stories. In one he is even called Don Enrique, like Henry Emmunds, who is also called Enrique in "The Denunciation." In both he lives in the Hotel Florida and in both "the girl" is referred to as "rabbit" (KL/EH 522a; 824). To anyone who has any experience with the Hemingway manuscripts, there can be very little doubt that this female character, called "rabbit," is based on Martha Gellhorn.

That sort of fictional procedure is not atypical for Hemingway's females. Catherine Barkley in *A Farewell to Arms* was clearly based in part on Agnes von Kurowsky, yet the experience of the caesarean operation came from his then wife Pauline's delivery of their son Patrick. Hemingway tended to create composite females, especially in love stories. As Patrick humorously claimed in a *USA Today* interview when the posthumous novel *The Garden of Eden* was published, the female characters in that book were "based on every single woman that my father ever knew. And there were quite a few of them."[10]

In María's case, however, the most fascinating element is the element of imagination, quite the opposite of Hemingway's technique with Pilar. Stanton believes, as I do, that overly realistic readings of María, or the criticism that she is too passive, miss the point, and he places her instead in the context of nature:

> . . . her hair has the golden color of ripe wheat, her face, skin, and eyes are the same tawny brown as the Castilian earth. . . . Her parents have been murdered, her village sacked, she has been violated as Spain herself has been pillaged and raped by foreign and native soldiers for centuries. (Stanton, 175)

Stanton believes, finally, that via his union with María, Jordan, "the American, has achieved his supreme symbolic union with Spain, the Spanish earth and people" (Stanton, 175).

John J. Teunissen, who gives the novel one of its deepest readings so far, believes the union between Robert and María is an example of "hierogamy," a term meaning literally "sacred union." I believe with him that Jordan's quest in Spain is, as was Hemingway's, essentially spiritual or sacred. As a result, " . . . the impulse to seek union with María in a sleeping bag under the stars is in Robert Jordan a primitive and religious one. For María, whose cropped hair is like a beaver pelt or a field of grain and who walks like a colt *is* Robert Jordan's America, his new found land," or, I might add, his undiscovered country (Teunissen, 233; for the body of the lover as "America" and "new-found-land," read John Donne's Elegy 19, "Going to Bed").

In a footnote, Teunissen adds that, while critical opinion—which he is going against—is almost unanimous in believing María to be the weakest character in the novel, what Hemingway was really after is not realism at all but "the numenal" (Teunissen, 237), that is, the divine, the holy, the spiritual, the mystery within. (The adjective is usually numinous, so that is the form I will use). María's name, I think, only emphasizes this quality in her.

We will analyze the love scenes later, but for now we should remember that we always see María as a projection of Robert Jordan, through Jordan's eyes. She is, in fact, very much like Jung's concept of the anima, which is to say the personification of Jordan's own feminine nature that he, consciously or unconsciously, seeks. His quest for her, like all quests, is essentially sacred and its "object" is numinous. María is, as Jordan thinks,

> . . . my true love and my wife. I never had a true love. I never had a wife. She is also my sister, and I never had a sister, and my daughter, and I never will have a daughter. (381)

As Teunissen comments, "This is not . . . sentimental. It emerges from and strikes back down into the most basic and primitive yearnings of mankind, yearnings which primitive man seeks to realize through myth and ritual and which the modern artist occasionally expresses through his art" (Teunissen, 234).

María: daughter, sister, lover, wife. María is not sentimental or passive or the projection of a fantasy, as some critics have claimed. She is a numinous figure, the shining incarnation of Robert Jordan's other half. To see her as anything less is to miss the basic mystery of love that is one of the novel's greatest achievements, but the discussion of that mystery must wait until we examine the action itself.

Robert Jordan's origins have caused a good deal of speculation, often erroneous. In 1966 Cecil D. Eby published an article called "The Real Robert Jordan," in which he proceeded to tell us that Major Robert Merriman, a former economics teacher at Berkeley who had become the highest ranking American volunteer in Spain, "provided a working model for the portrait of Robert Jordan in *For Whom the Bell Tolls*."[11] In actual fact, Robert Jordan owed little or nothing to the Lincoln Brigade commander, even though Hemingway knew him up to his death near Gandesa in the battle of the Ebro in April 1938 and wrote about his heroic exploits, as did Martha Gellhorn and others. Jeffrey Meyers is closer to the truth when he comments in opposition to Eby's article that " . . . apart from their first names and nationality, and the fact that they both fought and died in Spain, Merriman and Jordan have nothing in common" (Meyers 1988, 15).

Actually they did have one other thing in common: both were communists, after a fashion. Merriman wrote "Long live communism!" in his diary (Wyden, 284). The writer Robert Blair Kaiser, who was once to have co-authored a book on Merriman, read Merriman's entire diary and confirmed to me in San Diego in March 1987 that on the first Saturday of May 1937 Merriman joined the Communist party in Spain.

Robert Jordan was a communist, too, up through the novel's galleys, and then in response to an objection from Charles Scribner, Hemingway decided to remove the one passage in which Jordan admits that he had been a communist for two years (*Letters*, 512). He replaced "communist" with "anti-fascist" (KL/EH 86, galley 21; *FWTBT*, 66). Jordan should probably have been a communist—most of the volunteers were—but Hemingway made it politically cleaner for American readers by deciding to make him explicitly not a communist, but an antifascist instead. Even if Jordan had remained a communist, however, he would have been no less critical and no less heroic, and Hemingway almost surely made him a nominal communist only for the sake of realism. The removal of the word changed his putative affiliation, but it did not alter his critical nature one whit.

Whatever similarities he may or may not have shared with Merriman, Jordan had many of the personal characteristics and opin-

Martha Gellhorn, Spanish Civil War correspondent for *Collier's*, partial model for Maria, and after the war, Mrs. Ernest Hemingway; and Major Robert Merriman, the highest ranking American volunteer in Spain, once considered a model for Robert Jordan. Probably taken in April 1937.

Courtesy of the Hemingway Collection, John F. Kennedy Library. (Photo no. EH4692P).

ions of his author. Jordan's situation in Spain was very different from Hemingway's, but his personality is closer to Hemingway's than any of the other major protagonists except Nick Adams in the early stories.

Much has been written about Hemingway's heroes—perhaps I should write Hemingway's Heroes—but much of that criticism is misleading. In fact the word *hero* is misleading. Nick Adams is perhaps a nascent hero, an initiate still in his early period of learning about fear. Jake Barnes in *The Sun Also Rises* is no hero—he is a tragic victim, the insider. Frederic Henry in *A Farewell to Arms* is a deserter and a tragic outsider. Harry Morgan in *To Have and Have Not* is another victim and a pariah to boot. Harry in "The Snows of Kilimanjaro" hates himself for *not* being a hero, for having given in to easy money. Francis Macomber in his story is only a kind of hero for an instant, and then he too becomes a tragic victim. The first real hero in Hemingway's fiction—someone who sacrifices himself (all the way, if necessary) for something larger (the cause), or for someone else (María and the band)—is Robert Jordan.

I am not saying, by the way, that Jordan *is* Hemingway. He clearly is not, but he is made up from inside Hemingway and shares a great deal with him. In the next chapter we'll look at Jordan's actions—what they are and where they came from—and in so doing we will see how the plot and his character are parallel.

In the meantime we can end by remembering that, to get Jordan whole, Hemingway had to make him "people." For a while, Jordan, in a totally unintended irony, was that noble communist Hemingway had warned Dos Passos about, at least until Hemingway edited that from the galley. Did he have the habits Hemingway had ascribed to such a noble communist? Here's what Hemingway wrote to Max Perkins about the galleys:

> I fixed the Onan so it would not bother Charley I hope. After all Robert Jordan is a man and the idea of holding someone all night in your arms that you had intercourse with normally, on a night before an attack when he wanted to go to sleep would bring up some sort of a problem. I tried to handle his *rejection* of one solution of the problem delicately. If it is repulsive to several people

to whom you show it, I can cut it out. But remember it is by the small things of that sort that the man becomes absolutely credible instead of just a Hero. (*Letters*, 513-14; my emphasis; *FWTBT*, 342; in galleys Robert Jordan also rejected that solution, although the wording was more graphic, KL/EH 86, galley 104.)

10

The Action: Day One

In the introduction to his anthology *Men at War* (1942), Hemingway wrote: "A writer's job is to tell the truth. His standard of fidelity to the truth should be so high that his invention, out of his experience, should produce a truer account than anything factual can be. For facts can be observed badly; but when a good writer is creating something, he has time and scope to make it of an absolute truth."[1]

Earl Rovit, calling *For Whom the Bell Tolls* Hemingway's "most ambitious novel," believes that among many other ambitions, and "beyond all these," the book is "a struggle to cast a personal metaphor of his unique vision of life."[2]

Combining Hemingway's and Rovit's observations, we can say that the absolute truth of fiction cast as personal metaphor becomes the driving force behind *For Whom the Bell Tolls*. Robert Jordan's character forces the action of the novel and Hemingway's vision of life controls Robert Jordan. To reverse that, Hemingway creates Robert Jordan and Robert Jordan causes the action of the novel. Jordan is not Hemingway, remember, but he is very much *of* Hemingway.

The setting is circular; Jordan's life as we know it—as Hemingway put it, "he has all his life in those days" (*Letters*, 514)—is circular, from pine-needled earth to pine-needled earth; and as Rovit and Baker and other critics have observed, the plot is circular. That is because all are part of that larger personal metaphor, which is also circular.

Rovit may have the most succinct summary of the plot: "Jordan arrives with his orders at Pablo's cave, makes his arrangements, falls in love with María, has a slight obstructional deterrence from Pablo, explodes the bridge on schedule, and prepares to die when his broken leg makes it impossible for him to escape" (Rovit, 141). Notice that Jordan is the subject of all those verbs, and keep in mind what Hemingway told his friend Ben Finney when, after reading the unfinished manuscript in Cuba, Finney insisted that Hemingway must have "personally experienced the action" related in the novel: "Hell no [said Hemingway]. I made it up" (Baker 1969, 347).

Carlos Baker has pointed out some of Hemingway's personal characteristics and opinions that were passed on to Jordan:

> Jordan's parents were clearly modeled on Dr. and Mrs. Hemingway. The elder Jordan had shot himself to death with a Smith and Wesson Civil War pistol. His son was made to reflect on his father's cowardice . . . and his mother's aggressiveness . . . (Baker 1969, 348).

There are many other similarities we could point out, such as Jordan's temper, yet it is perhaps more instructive to wonder where the differences came from since the similarities seem quite obvious.

Baker has also given us the best description of the circular nature of the plot. Employing Jordan's own word, he called it "the wheel." Commenting on Jordan's musings about the nature of "the wheel" that his conflict with Pablo has occasioned in chapter eighteen, Baker wrote,

> Call it the wheel of human conflict. For Jordan, as for all men, the turn of the wheel shows tragic implications. When it has completed its revolution, the rider is back where he started. . . . In the giant clockwork of human relations, the turning wheels may be as small as the arguments with Pablo, or as vast as the elliptical rise and fall in the action of a year of war.

In either of these instances, in three days or three years, you come
back to where you began—"and nothing is settled." This is the
wheel-like turn of Spain's tragedy, indeed, that after all the agony
and all the blood, nothing should be settled, and that Spain
should be back where it began, in a medieval situation. (Baker
1972, 262–63)

Bearing these ideas in mind, let us spin out the action of the
novel to see what we find on this great wheel of three days and nights
and a fourth morning. But let us remember Jordan's comments on the
nature of the wheel as we go:

It is a vast wheel, set at an angle, and each time it goes around and
then is back to where it starts. One side is higher than the other
and the sweep it makes lifts you back and down to where you
started. . . . There is only one turn; one large, elliptical, rising and
falling turn and you are back where you have started. (225)

Such a wheel suggests many things, not least of which is the elliptical orbit of the earth itself. Its revolutions—the sun also ariseth, and
the sun goeth down—mark days, years, lifetimes, from which there is
no escape (as the preacher in Ecclesiastes who gave Hemingway the
title for *The Sun Also Rises* so well knew) except, perhaps, momentarily in this novel. Jordan is on the wheel—the big elliptical wheel—as we
all are. In his three days and three nights and one morning, in this
short period that is "all of his life," he rides the wheel once around
from Spanish earth to Spanish earth. But once or twice he manages to
get off that wheel. That one glorious moment or two makes the ride
worthwhile, and it marks the highest point, the zenith, of
Hemingway's personal metaphor of his unique vision of life.

Let's ride the wheel of three days and three nights and a fourth
morning with Robert Jordan to see if we can understand how in that
short time he can have "all his life." Actually it is slightly less than
three full days, from afternoon of the first day until before noon of the
fourth. A review of the novel's action is necessary for revealing
Hemingway's unique vision and for understanding his complex use of
irony, which is not always discernible on one reading.

The Action: Day One

The novel begins sometime in the afternoon of Day One (chapters 1–7) with Robert Jordan lying "flat on the brown, pine-needled floor of the forest" (1). Jordan is with Anselmo, looking at the pass and the stream alongside the road and the new mill. Anselmo tells him that below, out of sight, the terrain drops suddenly and that there is a steep gorge with a bridge over it. This landscape already does not correspond to the real pass at all. We are, from the first paragraph, in the undiscovered country of Hemingway's imagination.

Since we have already seen that there were no guerrillas, much less "more than a hundred" (2) as Anselmo tells Jordan, and that this country between Navacerrada and the "old mill" (1) down at Valsaín near La Granja, was not "behind the enemy lines" (4), we can now dispense with reality and move behind the lines in the far country of Hemingway's "absolute truth."

After a flashback in which Jordan remembers the scene with General Golz in which he got his orders to blow the bridge to prevent the advance of Nationalist (fascist) troops against the "surprise" offensive by the Loyalist army on La Granja and Segovia (6), Jordan and Anselmo meet Pablo and proceed to the guerrilla camp, stopping to inspect the all-important horses. Pablo asks Jordan a question about his having had to shoot his fellow guerrilla, the Russian Kashkin, which we now see as heavily freighted with significance: "If you are wounded in such a thing as this bridge, you would be willing to be left behind [rather than being shot like Kashkin]?" (21).

Jordan does not answer this question that presages the rest of the novel, because "the girl," as she is called in the idiom of the time, appears:

> Her teeth were white in her brown face and her skin and eyes were the same golden tawny brown. Her hair was the golden brown of a grain field that has been burned dark in the sun but it was cut short all over her head so that it was but little longer than the fur on a beaver pelt. (22)

The appearance of the girl banishes the question of death. Jordan, instantly affected by María, falls in love with her without yet realizing it, and she falls in love with him—only she knows it, as we learn later that night when she tells him, "I loved you when I saw you today . . . " (73). This apparent "love at first sight" goes far deeper than some unimaginative critics realized, and Hemingway took pains in the dialogue between María and Robert to reveal this depth. María continues the sentence above with these words: " . . . and I loved you *always* but I never saw you before . . . " (73; my emphasis). If you mistake this for just romantic talk, you miss Hemingway's main reason for writing *For Whom the Bell Tolls*, which is first and foremost a love story, Hemingway's greatest love story, for it was from love—and only from love—that his unique vision emanated.

Before the love can develop fully, however, other darker forces must present themselves, such as María's condition at the time of her discovery when the train was blown; Jordan's wondering if the Gypsy Rafael can "read in the palm of my hand and tell me what is going to pass in the next three days" (27); and the Gypsy's description of the blowing of the train when the earth moves for the first time—in death:

> . . . and then, at the moment of the explosion, the front wheels of the engine rose up and *all of the earth seemed to rise* in a great cloud of blackness and a roar and the engine rose high in the cloud of dirt and of the wooden ties rising in the air as in a dream and then it fell onto its side like a great wounded animal. . . . (29; my emphasis)

Then, like one of the pre-Christian Iberian idols that inspired Picasso's early cubism, Pilar appears with her "brown face like a model for a granite monument" (30). She reads Jordan's hand but will tell him nothing of what she sees there. All the main characters involved in the foreground action have now appeared, and along with them the forces in contention have also gathered: war, death, love, and fate.

Anselmo and Jordan inspect the bridge, make plans for blowing it, and compare Gypsies and American Indians, both of whom "believe the bear to be a brother to man" (40). Anselmo reveals himself, rather like Santiago in *The Old Man and the Sea*, to be a lover of nature and a man of true inner dignity and nobility. Yet he should not be taken for a "noble savage," for he is far more complex than that. Although he is not a Gypsy and does not say the bear is his brother (as Santiago does with the marlin), still the clear suggestion that he reveres nature as they do places him more in the world of folk wisdom than in that of the mythical noble savage. One detail subtly emphasizes this role. "On the door of the church of my village was nailed the paw of a bear that I killed . . . ," Anselmo tells Jordan (39).

Anselmo is from the town of Barco de Avila on the edge of the Gredos Mountains. Did Anselmo have a model there? Perhaps. In 1931 Hemingway wrote somewhat cryptically to John Dos Passos, "Barco de Avila is wonderful town. Killed a wolf there while we were there. Bear paw nailed to door of church . . . " (*Letters*, 342). Anselmo's wisdom and dependability, important to establish, counter Pablo's treachery and bouts of cowardice.

Jordan, in a pensive mood, first resents "Golz's orders, and the necessity of them," and then, typically, calls himself to task and realizes one of the central assumptions of the novel, that "the bridge can be the point on which the future of the human race can turn" (43). Notice, too, that Jordan thinks, "can" be and "can" turn, not necessarily *will* be and *will* turn.

In the evening, inside the cave, Jordan and Pablo have their confrontation: Jordan comes close to killing Pablo, and Pablo relinquishes power to Pilar. In that process Pilar relates how her former companion, the *torero* Finito, had reacted when gored, spinning out a whole story in which she plays both herself and Finito in a comic and grotesque narration that ends with Finito, played by Pilar, recounting his goring:

> Pilar, it is nothing. It shouldn't have happened. I killed him very well, you understand. Nobody could have killed him better. Then having killed him exactly as I should and him absolutely dead, swaying on his legs, and ready to fall of his own weight, I walked away from him with a certain amount of arrogance and much style and from the back he throws me this horn between the cheeks of my buttocks and it comes out of my liver. (55)

Some critics have objected to this kind of blood-and-guts episode in the novel, but it forms a natural enough part of the Spain Hemingway was trying to represent. As Arturo Barea has objected, it may do some small injustice to the Castilian villagers to have to be subject to these affairs of Pilar, but in a larger way—just as when he placed Pilar and María in Castilla even though they were, in fact, based on Andalusian women—Hemingway was representing all of Spain in his mountain microcosm. Remember that he told Malcolm Cowley, "But it wasn't just the civil war I put into it . . . it was everything I had learned about Spain for eighteen years" (*Life*, 10 January 1949).

To verify that passage, consider that on 30 August 1985 in Colmenar Viejo, a town north of Madrid and just south of the Guadarrama mountains where *For Whom the Bell Tolls* takes place, José Cubero Sánchez, a promising young matador called *El Yiyo*, went in for the kill on the sixth and final bull of the afternoon and placed a good sword between the bull's withers. The mortally wounded bull tripped Yiyo, catching him from behind, higher up than Finito's wound in the buttocks and liver, and ran his horn into the twenty-one-year-old matador's heart, throwing him to the ground, then standing him up. As he came off the horn, the torero spoke his last words to his assistant, "This bull has killed me." Then he collapsed, arriving dead at the infirmary.

As Federico García Lorca once remarked, "Spain is the only country where death is the national spectacle, where death sounds long trumpets at the arrival of springtime."[3] Hemingway was, of course, supremely aware of Spain's consciousness of death, and he deliberately explored death and related themes such as goring, pain, suffering, killing, and suicide in *For Whom the Bell Tolls*, despite the squeamishness of some of his critics.

The first day ends with Pablo deposed, Jordan accepted by the members of the band, and Pilar firmly in control. Her first decision is to send María, who is anything but unwilling, out to Robert Jordan's "sleeping robe," that "was spread on the forest floor in the lee of the rocks beyond the cave mouth" (69). Barea, among others, has objected to such behavior, but to do so raises again the objection of realism, which can only pale alongside the urgency of Hemingway's telescoped vision of all of life in three days. Of course it is not "realistic," but *For Whom the Bell Tolls* is not a "realistic" novel. It is a passionate love story in which two lovers must live out their lives together in a few hours. As Hemingway expressed it to Scott Fitzgerald in 1925, " . . . war is the best subject of all. It groups the maximum of material and speeds up the action and brings out all sorts of stuff that normally you have to wait a lifetime to get" (*Letters*, 176).

The situation of war compounds the urgency of the passion of María and Robert, which is as rare as all such passions. In such a union, the sacred union of perfect and fulfilling love, there is no such thing as appropriate behavior, especially under the circumstances. All behavior is appropriate and all things are, for the first time in their lives, possible. Pilar senses this and she tells María that if they "do everything together, the other maybe never will have been" (72). Only love can heal María, as Pilar understands. And Pilar also knows that time is short. Day One closes, not unlike a movie of the period, with suggestion:

> "And now let us do quickly what it is we do so that the other is all gone."
> "You want?"
> "Yes," she said almost fiercely. "Yes. Yes. Yes." (73)

Hemingway, like James Joyce in Molly Bloom's soliloquy in *Ulysses*, understood the urgent sexuality implicit in the soft, suppliant sibilance of yeses. Fade to black.

11

The Action: Day Two

Day Two (chapters 8–20) begins as the fascist planes fly over, "hammering the sky apart" (75). Jordan visualizes them crossing beyond the pass with "the shadows of the Heinkels moving over the land as the shadows of sharks pass over a sandy floor of the ocean" (76). "They can't know about the attack, he told himself and something in him said, why can't they? They've known about all the others" (77). These are two of the major enemies of the Republic: Hitler's air force and betrayal from within. When solemn Fernando arrives from La Granja, he confirms Nationalist reports of the offensive, "One here and the other over the Alto del León near the Escorial," precisely the two passes, Navacerrada and Alto del León on the other road to Segovia, where the historical offensive was aimed.

In actual fact, too visible troop movement and desertions—particularly by one sergeant who evidently crossed into Nationalist territory on the night of 29 May 1937 with detailed plans of the preparations—were largely responsible for the lack of surprise in the offensive.[1] In the novel Fernando has even heard talk "that the Republicans would try to blow up the bridges" (82), while in fact no bridges were blown in the real offensive, an obviously unwise stratagem since, as we've seen, the bridge in question was not behind the lines.

Hemingway used interesting and telling juxtapositions in *For Whom the Bell Tolls*, alternating here, for example, the flight of the planes and Pilar's narrative of her glory days with Finito in Valencia. Hemingway had been often to the July *Feria* in Valencia and was fond of the city. His descriptions remind me of the luminous beachscapes painted by the Valencian Impressionist Joaquín Sorolla. Pilar says, "We went to the beach and lay in the water and boats with sails were hauled up out of the sea by oxen. . . . Ten yokes of oxen dragging a boat with sails out of the sea in the morning with the line of the small waves breaking on the beach. That is Valencia." That and the *"paella* with fresh sea food, clams in their shells, mussels, crayfish and small eels" (84–85). These descriptions of Valencia also resemble the elegiac last chapter of *Death in the Afternoon*, describing a Spain that no longer existed in 1932.

Just as Pilar finishes, "they heard the first sound of the planes returning" (86). As the planes get closer, "beating the sky apart with the noise of their motors," Jordan thinks,

> "They *are* shaped like sharks . . . the wide-finned, sharp-nosed sharks of the Gulf Stream. But these, wide-finned in silver, roaring, the light mist of their propellers in the sun, these do not move like sharks. They move like no thing there has ever been. They move like mechanized doom." (87)

The Spain of those days, the juxtaposition seems to indicate, is finished forever and their mechanized doom is brought about by the coming and going of the Luftwaffe, which was in the spring of 1937 experimenting with the technique of the deliberate bombing of civilian populations in Spain, including the Condor Legion's infamous market-day massacre at the sacred Basque town of Guernica just a month before (26 April 1937). We should not forget that this completely deliberate attack, including the machine-gunning of the fleeing civilian population, was the single most discussed incident in the Spanish Civil War (absurdly, first the Nationalists and then Catholic spokesmen worldwide denied the aerial attack), a discussion magnificently underscored by Picasso's epochal painting, *Guernica*.

The planes inspire dread in Pilar, who remarks, "We are nothing against such machines" (89). They make her very conscious of the importance of time: "I am no coward, but I see things very clearly in the early morning and I think there are many that we know that are alive now who will never see another Sunday" (89), a dread she reiterates to Jordan in urging him to seize every opportunity to make love to María: "There is not much time" (91). We see that love and death, especially sexual love and death, like two sides of the same coin, are in constant juxtaposition and flux. As Pilar says, "You have the night, but there is the day, too. Clearly there is no such luxury as in Valencia in my time. But you could pick a few wild strawberries . . . " (92).

In chapter ten, Pilar, Robert Jordan, and María go to see El Sordo. Pilar stops along the way to wash her feet in a stream and tell her horrible and fascinating tale of "the day of revolution in a small town where all know all in the town and always have known all" (106). The revolution takes place in a nameless Castilian village possibly somewhere near Avila, the intentionally nameless home of Pablo (and possibly of Pilar, too, although Pilar's actual provenance or even province are never really pinned down). The revolution in Pablo's town clearly stands for conflict in any and all such small towns involved in the violent and unyielding class struggle so central to the Spanish Civil War (Spain had had no class war such as the French Revolution).

This scene of brutal massacre—committed by those on the side of the Republic—drew heavy fire from the political Left in the U.S. and was interpreted as a traitorous depiction of events. At the meeting with the Veterans of the Abraham Lincoln Brigade, Hemingway defended himself, claiming, according to Alvah Bessie, that it "was a true incident of the war" (Bessie, 14).

Was it a "true incident of the war"? As is so often the case, the answer is both yes and no. Hemingway apparently told Hotchner in 1954, "When Pilar remembers back to what happened in their village when the Fascists came, that's Ronda, and the details of the town are exact" (Hotchner, 131). Hugh Thomas judges Hemingway's description as "near to the reality of what happened in the famous Andalusian town of Ronda (though the work was the responsibility of a gang from Málaga). There 512 were murdered in the first month of the war" (Thomas, 274).

Hemingway clearly had privileged access to many of the horror stories of the war. He knew about Ronda, and he certainly knew of the massacres by the Nationalists in the bullring at Badajoz because Jay Allen, who reported the story, was a close friend. In the early stages of the war some nearly unimaginable massacres occurred on both sides. Bessie's notion that such massacres were "extremely sporadic in Republican territory" and that they were the "policy of the fascist forces" (Bessie, 14–15), sounds ingenuous at best. The grand old dean of Hispanophiles, Gerald Brenan, may have had the last word when he commented on the Andalusian town of Guadix where young terrorists committed many murders, only to be followed by even fiercer Nationalist purges at the end of the war: "One may take it as a rule that in class wars it is the side that wins that kills most."[2]

Hotchner's report notwithstanding, the details of the town are far from exact. In fact the only real similarities between Ronda and the town of the novel's massacre are the cliff and the river below, a magnificent site that Hemingway obviously found perfect, even though it meant transferring it—as with María and Pilar—from Andalucía to Castilla. Hemingway was probably more accurate about what he actually did when he described the process years later (1954) to his friend Bernard Berenson:

> We are old enough to try to talk truly and I tell you this only as a curiosity. A few other things which I *invented completely* such as the story in "For Whom the Bell Tolls" of Pablo and Pilar and their doing away with the fascists in the village, I read, when by chance I have to do it, with complete astonishment that I could have *invented it* as I did. You know that fiction, prose rather, is possibly the roughest trade of all in writing. . . . You have the sheet of blank paper, the pencil, and *the obligation to invent truer than things can be true.* You have to take what is not palpable and make it completely palpable and also have it seem normal and so that it can become a part of the experience of the person who reads it. (*Letters*, 837; my emphasis)

The finest critical interpretations of this palpable episode come from Robert E. Gajdusek and H. R. Stoneback. Gajdusek has examined the moment of revolution in the light of the philosophy of Nietzsche and the psychology of Jung as the overthrow of the masculine, solar, authoritarian, Apollonian forces by the feminine, lunar, revolutionary, Dionysian uprising. He describes this process as a

> destructive activity that is coevally creative . . . a fertility ritual in which fertility is assured through the separation of the chaff from the wheat, through the threshing and harvesting rituals in which the act of killing with sickle and scythe, or turning or tumbling with a wooden pitchfork, is part of a death process out of which comes renewed life.[3]

Gajdusek's article reveals great complexity of construction, and the deep psychological implications he sees in this "tale" argue very strongly for an intentional, and therefore invented, structure.

Stoneback's piece concerns the price paid in human suffering for the revolution and centers on the figure of the priest, the only priest in the novel, "as the real focus of the tale . . . for Pilar in the act of telling, for Pablo in the act of participating and for Hemingway in the precisely crafted act of writing." Even for Pablo, "who hates priests worse than he hates fascists," or perhaps because of that, "everything, the very essence of Spain, is at stake in the death of a Spanish priest." Stoneback believes Pilar's tale, as indeed "everything in *For Whom the Bell Tolls*, conspires to affirm and to take the reader to the heart of [Anglican priest] Donne's meditation." The epigraph of the novel is "not at all concerned with some superficial leftist vision of brotherhood . . . but with the core Christian vision of the oneness of humankind and the relationship of the individual soul to fate." It is important, I believe, to hear Stoneback on this matter. Pablo knows even in his drunken stupor (and that is why he drinks), and Pilar knows (and that is why she recounts) the truth of the epigraph, that regardless of the necessities of war, as Stoneback phrases it, "every death diminishes everyone, and the complicity, for all of Spain and for everyone involved spreads beyond mere knowing, demands—as that rare Christian Anselmo insists—expiation and penance."[4]

Here is Stoneback's conclusion, well worth our consideration:

> As George Orwell observed in *Homage to Catalonia*: "The sin of nearly all left-wingers from 1933 onwards is that they have wanted to be anti-Fascist without being anti-totalitarian." As Pilar's tale demonstrates, Hemingway does not commit that sin in *For Whom the Bell Tolls*. The novel's ultimate vision approaches that profound and elusive, tragic and redemptive knowledge which declares the need for expiation in the life of communities and nations, a need which has been promulgated in and by all of the outrageous and paradoxical Tiananmen Squares of our bloody century. In Madrid as in Beijing, in all places and times and most especially in our century so ravaged by politics, our epoch so devastated by statism, murderous dogmatism, and isms of every kind, the free, volitional act of resistance to the gnostic rage of ideology—of the left or of the right—must be linked, as Anselmo and Pilar and Hemingway know, as Solzhenitsyn and certain contemporary Chinese writers know, with communal sacraments of atonement. (Stoneback, 15)

As if to prove Stoneback's point, Pablo, remembering his victims later, will say, "If I could restore them to life, I would" (209).

Far from Alvah Bessie's simplistic claim in 1970 that "The Spanish war was one of the purest and most easily understood conflicts of modern times" (Bessie, 15), Hemingway's profound understanding of that complex conflict and of its historically gruesome scapegoatism prefigured and shaped his "obligation to invent truer than things can be true." It was never, for Hemingway the novelist, a question of propaganda or the correct political posture. To the extent that Gajdusek and Stoneback are right, Pilar's tale not only "represents the working out of certain spiritual and political dilemmas which gave him great anguish in the late 1930s" (Stoneback, 15), it actually incarnates in an intentionally grisly and realistic fashion some of the novel's deepest psychological and spiritual insights, insights that are underscored precisely by virtue of their occurrence on the "wrong" side. To see the scene as politics—or as sensationalism—misses the whole point. It is, as Capellán has remarked, "a supra-reality, a symbolic—but not less realistic—expression of the tragedy of the Spanish Civil War" (Capellán, 265).

Beautifully phrased, almost poetic at times, and always grim in its realism and taurine symbolism (not unlike Picasso's *Guernica*), Pilar's tale also becomes a self-conscious and intentional analogue for the novel as a whole. Cruelty and drunkenness and shame and the unruly animal of mob behavior—with their precise counterpoint in Jordan's account of the Ohio lynching of the black man—belong to no one group or to no one nation's patrimony. Jordan thinks, going up to the camp of El Sordo, "Pilar had made him see it in that town. If that woman could only write. He would try to write it and if he had luck and could remember it perhaps he could get it down as she told it. God, how she could tell a story. She's better than Quevedo, he thought" (134). He is inviting us—unintentionally from his own point of view, but intentionally from Hemingway's—to experience the novel as he has experienced Pilar's tale, seeing it as though we had actually been present. For her part, when she finishes her account, Pilar, who for Jordan "is like a mountain" (136), and whom he calls "a psychiatrist," says that the afternoon will come, "It will come flying and go the same way and tomorrow will fly, too" (130), reminding us yet again of the stifling lack of time.

El Sordo and his caves in "these limestone upper basins" (138) are another Hemingway invention, for no such limestone upper basins exist—and El Sordo himself is a fine invention at that. Stanton has pointed out that his real name, Santiago, is that of the Patron of Spain and that his *nom de guerre*, El Sordo, may be a reference to one of Hemingway's favorite painters, Francisco de Goya, who was deaf in his later days (Stanton, 179). El Sordo, who hears a lot for a deaf man, brings more bad news from Segovia: the offensive is known, and there is heavy movement of troops toward the bridge. Also El Sordo points out what is lacking besides time: horses. El Sordo, a grand guerrilla fighter, represents everything that Pablo is not, and he makes quite clear to Jordan the difficulty of getting out alive after blowing the bridge in daylight.

Coming back from El Sordo's camp, in the high meadow on the late May afternoon, Robert Jordan and María make love. The first time they make love, we are not allowed to know what happens. But this time the earth moves and we know all about it.

What does it mean that the earth moves? Now is the time to consider the profound significance of that figure of speech, for it leads us eventually to the deepest level of meaning of the novel. For the most part the critics have skirted the issue of its meaning. Stanton twice thinks it is "the ecstasy of orgasm" (171, 177), but Teunissen disagrees:

> This *hierogamous* union has great efficacy for the lovers who "feel the earth move" (p. 160) and as a result of which they pass into "*la gloria*" (p. 379). The earth's moving is what for Pilar sets the *sacred seal* upon the union: for it never moves more than three times in any lifetime, and for most people—the profane ones—it moves not at all. This evidence of hierogamy is gypsy knowledge and, as Pilar makes clear, *it is not a primitive euphemism for orgasm.* (Teunissen, 234; my emphasis)

Hierogamy, remember, means a sacred, as opposed to a profane, which is to say normal, union. *La gloria*, about which we will say more in a moment, is the way María describes their lovemaking, both in chapter thirty-seven, when she actually says it, and here in chapter ten. It is an intentionally religious, albeit popular, expression. Most important of all, it does not simply mean orgasm.

Hemingway did not have much to say on the subject. Baker reports that he became uncomfortable while speaking with a group of professors in Hawaii, and "defended his metaphor of the moving earth in Jordan's love scenes with María" (Baker 1969, 359).

His most telling comment came in a letter to William Faulkner in 1947. Faulkner had commented to some students at the University of Mississippi about his own doctrine of splendid failure (having no idea a reporter was present) and put Hemingway at the bottom of the list, after Dos Passos, Thomas Wolfe, Erskine Caldwell, and himself, "because he [Hemingway] lacked the courage to get out on a limb of experimentation" (Baker 1969, 461). Hemingway felt insulted when the comments were picked up and published by the Associated Press, Faulkner apologized, and Hemingway wrote to Faulkner about his willingness to experiment, giving as his prime example,

... like when they are fucking comeing back from making contact with the other outfit about the bridge, when the Pilar woman knows what the hell it is all about. ... (*Letters*, 624)

Hemingway's near pidgin English, his peculiarly faulty spelling, and his obscenity only point up his sensitivity over this matter. But isn't it interesting that he picks that particular scene to illustrate his experimentation *and* includes the fact that Pilar "knows what the hell it is all about"? He also told Faulkner that this (and some other examples, including Pilar's tale of the massacre and the "smell of death" passage) "is as good as I can write and was takeing all chances . . . could take" (*Letters*, 624). No, we can safely conclude that there is something here a good deal more complex than "the ecstacy of orgasm," although a special kind of ecstasy is indeed what it is about, and it does occur as they reach the climax of their lovemaking. Keep in mind that ecstasy for Hemingway has a special religious connotation that we will examine shortly.

The trajectory of love in Hemingway's work is toward this special ecstasy. The impossibility of such love runs all through *The Sun Also Rises*. It begins for real and ends tragically when Catherine dies in childbirth in *A Farewell to Arms*. Then in *The Green Hills of Africa*, a non-fiction book not seemingly about love, there appears an important description of ecstatic love: " . . . to have, and be, and live in, to possess now again for always, for that long sudden-ended always; *making time stand still*, sometimes so very still that afterwards you wait to hear it move, and it is slow in starting."[5]

The most revealing phrase in terms of ecstasy is "making time stand still," for escape from the trap of time is an essential quality of ecstasy. Time is an important subject in *Green Hills of Africa*, but it is paramount in *For Whom the Bell Tolls*. The three days and nights and the final fourth morning all determine in their inexorable telescoping, as we have begun to see, the nature of love, of life, of death, in short of everything in the novel. In fact, I can think of no more time-obsessed work, for time is the ground for all the undiscovered countries in *For Whom the Bell Tolls*. The mortal ticking, or I suppose I should say the tolling, begins in the book's title.

The Action: Day Two

In the first described instance of Robert and María's lovemaking, then, ecstasy involves stopping time. From at least *A Farewell to Arms* on, love is a religion for Hemingway. Catherine's famous phrase "You're my religion"[6] is straight from the rhetoric of courtly love and the literature of passion. María goes a step further and calls their lovemaking *la gloria*. And Jordan thinks, "La gloria. She said La Gloria. It has nothing to do with glory nor La Gloire that the French write and speak about. It is the thing that is in Cante Hondo and in the Saetas. It is in Greco and in San Juan de la Cruz, of course, and in the others" (380). *Saetas* are mystic religious flamenco songs, usually sung at Easterweek to the Virgin; El Greco was a mystic painter; San Juan de la Cruz, as we shall see, was a mystic poet, whose metaphor for mystical union was sexual.

Jordan is right. La gloria does not mean glory—it means heaven. María tells Jordan that she is thankful "to have been another time in *la gloria*" (379). *Estar en la gloria* means to be in heaven, to be out of this world, to be in ecstasy, in *ex-stasis*, that is, out of where one normally stands or is. It is, in short, sexual mysticism, sacred ecstasy, or what certain Buddhists would call tantric sexuality.

Robert and María make love four times. Only two are detailed love scenes: when the earth moves in the meadow on the afternoon of the second day, and in the early hours before the fourth and final morning. María says "another time," after the last love scene, so we can assume that both the scenes described refer to la gloria, even though the phrase itself occurs after the second description. Ecstasy then—the undiscovered country of love that neither of them had experienced before or had even known about—stops time and creates a mystical union María and Robert call in perfectly idiomatic Spanish *la gloria*.

But, is that it? Is there nothing new here, no further progression along the path of ecstasy? Hemingway had already described in *Green Hills of Africa* a certain kind of lovemaking that could stop time, and when Catherine and Frederic become in *A Farewell to Arms* "the same one" (*FTA*, 299), are we not dealing with a similar union? There is, I think, at least one more step, one more dimension involved in *For Whom the Bell Tolls*.

What does it mean when the earth moves? Is that a sympathetic response on Mother Earth's part? Is the great Indian earth-goddess Kali dancing in geopathic celebration? Is this the supreme pathetic fallacy, orgasm as earthquake? Or did Hemingway have something less overtly romantic in mind? The fact that the question "did the earth move for you?" has become a cultural cliché suggests that at a popular level the description is just corny romance of the kind that ends up in popular music such as Carole King's "I Feel the Earth Move." But Hemingway, ever so sensitive about these matters, surely had more in mind. What?

At the Hemingway Conference in Moscow in 1990 celebrating the fiftieth anniversary of the publication of *For Whom the Bell Tolls*, Professor Charles Oliver, then editor of the *Hemingway Review*, gave a very interesting paper comparing the language of the first of T. S. Eliot's *Four Quartets*, "Burnt Norton," to the language of love in *For Whom the Bell Tolls*. "Burnt Norton" is hardly a love scene, but as Oliver pointed out, the language is often similar, especially in its insistence on the *now*, the present.

After the Moscow meeting, phrases from "Burnt Norton" kept returning to me: "Time and the bell; And all is always now; Quick now, here, now, always;" and the epigraph from Heraclitus, "The way up and the way down are one and the same." Hemingway doubtless had read "Burnt Norton." The phrase—actually the paradox—that most titillated me was: "At the still point of the turning world . . . at the still point, there the dance is."[7] In terms of *For Whom the Bell Tolls*, I knew what the dance was, but was there some still point? And what could be a *still* point in a *turning* world?

After Einstein there was no still point anywhere in the universe. The only seeming stillness was constant speed. Lovers lying in a high Castilian meadow traveling at the same speed as the rotating earth—that might *seem* a still point in the turning world. And if they somehow stopped, the earth would go right on turning and "move out and away from under them" (159). Of course, it *was* Einstein. After Einstein there were no longer three dimensions of space and a separate one of time. After Einstein the fourth dimension, the famous fourth dimension, was space-time, no way to have one without the other. So the passage about "time absolutely still and they were both there, time having stopped and he felt the earth move out and away from under them" (159), was only logical; it made perfect sense, relatively speaking. It was a *modern* ecstasy, an escape for the sexually and spiritually bonded lovers, however momentary, from the continuum of *space*-time; not romance, not pathetic fallacy, not even Kali dancing. New physics. Or perhaps romance *and* religion *and* relativity. How to know?

Hemingway was certainly aware of Einstein's ideas. In the spring of 1921, before she became his first wife, Hadley Richardson used the phrase in a love letter to Hemingway, "an unknown fourth dimension just like ours."[8] And Michael Reynolds comments: "The idea of a fourth dimension was much discussed in those days, for Einstein's theories of relativity turned him into an international figure. . . . Years later when Hemingway needed a phrase to describe his art, he said he was trying to achieve in fiction a fourth dimension . . . which probably meant the *timeless* quality of great writing" (Reynolds 1986, 290; my emphasis). Reynolds is referring to *Green Hills of Africa* in which Hemingway says, speaking of writing, "There is a fourth and fifth dimension that can be gotten" (*GHA*, 27), but Hemingway never elaborated on these concepts.

In a later paper, "Einstein's Train Stops at Hemingway's Station," Reynolds looked at Hemingway's ironic treatment of time and space in the story "Homage to Switzerland," which was written in 1932. Reynolds had done his homework. He informs us that "from 1922–1928, the *New York Times* carried 172 stories about Einstein . . . and almost 100 articles appeared in English and American general periodicals."[9] Hemingway knew his Einstein all right, just the way he knew his Eliot and his Joyce and his Pound and his Stein, if by no other means than by osmosis: romance *and* religion *and* relativity.

It turns out that this combination is not strange, just somewhat advanced for its time, especially in Western culture. The earliest Eastern students of enlightenment found ecstasy through sexuality thousands of years ago. Ezra Pound and James Joyce were both interested—each in his own way, of course—in the connection. And sexual gurus, occultists, and mystics such as the Russians G. I. Gurdjieff and

P. D. Ouspensky, and their English counterparts, such as diabolist Aleister Crowley, whom Hemingway mentioned in *A Moveable Feast*, were common enough in Paris in the twenties. Ouspensky even talked about a circular fifth dimension, although it is not clear exactly what he meant. The French philosopher Henri Bergson discussed intuition, mysticism, and different kinds of time, especially intensity of experience, which he called "duration" as opposed to clock time; and Gertrude Stein, who admired Bergson, spoke of the "continuous present," which brings us back to "Burnt Norton" and *For Whom the Bell Tolls*.

Sexual ecstasy, sexual mysticism, and sex as religion were very much in the air. These were only new ideas to the children of sexually intolerant and repressive Western societies. And I do not mean just Joyce's Irish Catholicism or Hemingway's Oak Park Protestantism, but virtually the entire Western religious tradition. They were not exactly new ideas. San Juan de la Cruz's sixteenth-century metaphor for the mystical union or fusion of the soul with God was precisely the hierogamous physical union of two lovers who become one. This union was inspired by a similar union in the Song of Songs, which in turn drew its inspiration, as Biblical scholars have shown, from Near Eastern fertility rituals that were based on the idea of sacred sexuality. They were not new ideas; in fact for initiates they were very old, but they were daring enough in Hemingway's time and cultural context.

Hemingway's real stroke of genius was not his participation in this rediscovered ancient dance by virtue of his recognition that love could produce ecstasy, but the brilliant addition to that recognition of an image drawn from the physical world, from science, from relativity. Religion as love, androgyny, unity, sexual ecstasy, these topics fascinated Hemingway all his life, quite probably as early as his reading of Havelock Ellis's *The Psychology of Sex* in Chicago in 1920 (as my student Tracy Cox proved recently in a paper), more even than we had previously suspected until we read his posthumous novel, *The Garden of Eden*. But *For Whom the Bell Tolls* has something found nowhere else, for only here does the earth move.

A look once again at the passage from *Green Hills of Africa* helps us understand the importance of that addition: love can make "time stand still, sometimes so very still that afterwards you wait to hear it move, and it is slow in starting" (*GHA*, 72). Time stops, but only in a manner of speaking. The clever near-synaesthesia of hearing it move is not altogether convincing, nor is the oxymoronic phrase directly preceding the passage: "sudden-ended always." We are told, not shown. In Hemingway's terms, we do not experience the stopping of time. He does not make us feel it because he does not develop the description or provide a memorable image. It is flat, and flat passion, even flat talk about passion, no matter how poetically couched, is still flat.

On the other hand, *For Whom the Bell Tolls* provides us with an image. Personally, I see it as an image—the earth moving out from under them—within a larger design. The larger design is a yoni mandala. A mandala was originally a design within a circle used as an aid to meditation by Buddhists, but for Swiss psychologist Carl Gustav Jung it depicted the integration of the male and female halves of the self. The mandala here, my mandala, is a circle, and inside the circle is an upside down triangle, the symbol of the goddess of fertility, a delta. Inside the wheel, or the circle, from forest floor to forest floor we have the love story of Robert Jordan and María, which is the triangle of romance, religion, and relativity. It is upside down, a delta, a fertility sign, a yoni, because the way in becomes the way out; the in- of intercourse is the out, the ex-, of ecstasy. Ecstasy—to be *in* la gloria, *in* heaven, *in* bliss—and unity—"one and one is one, is one, is one . . . " (379)—come from the fusion of the sacred and the sexual—one and one is one, one body, one soul, the divine androgyne of classical mythology, Socrates' (and Jung's) two halves of the soul, male and female, united at last. Or as Jesus expressed it in the Gnostic gospel of Thomas, "When you make the male and the female one and the same . . . then you will enter [the kingdom]."[10]

The in becomes the out, the *ex* of ex-stasis and the effect is ecstasy—real ecstasy in *For Whom the Bell Tolls*, not rhetorical ecstasy as in *Green Hills of Africa* (and certainly not pedestrian biological orgasm). The lovers stop time as they become one, and of course the earth moves. While they climb the Jacob's ladder of tantric, that is, sexually heightened, consciousness to bliss, the world keeps on turning.[11] Pilar knows what it means because certain Gypsies preserve vestigial wisdom from their Indian past, and because a few of them live tantric, intuitive lives. That is, almost by definition, what hierogamy—sacred union—entails.

Intuition is perhaps the magic word. Does it matter if the earth actually moved (as opposed to their feeling that it did)? Does it matter if they were actually in la gloria (or only seemed to be)? Does it even matter if, in fact, Hemingway had relativity consciously in mind? Do we need to believe Hemingway could really deal in the arcane language of high mathematics? Is it not preferable to think of it as high poetics, high sexuality, and high romance? All language is, of course, metaphoric, but at the very least no overly literal physicist could come along and object. And no one ever forgets the earth's moving, which is why it has become a cliché—that magical moment of timelessness when the lovers are out of this world, passionately levitated above the gravity field of the mortal wheel they are riding down to death:

> . . . up, up, up and into nowhere, suddenly, scaldingly, holdingly all nowhere gone and time absolutely still and they were both there, time having stopped and he felt the earth move out and away from under them. (*FWTBT*, 159)

As Rebecca Fulcher, one of my students, observed recently in class, when time stops the "nowhere" turns into "now-here." Its very dizzying perfection as the core image from his unique vision of life is surely what made Hemingway sensitive about it. Is it any wonder that María calls it la gloria?

Hemingway's invented ecstasy for Robert Jordan and María had undeniably gotten the image right. Perhaps I should add that getting it right and then writing it right so that we experience it too, through his art, may be what Hemingway's fifth dimension in writing is about. Hemingway plays out the scene on the stage of his imagination and by getting it right—getting the words right, turning it into a kind of poetry in which the rhythm of the words recreates the rhythm of lovemaking—makes it play on the stage of the reader's imagination and makes it stay in the reader's memory.

The Action: Day Two

In *The Dancing Wu Li Masters: An Overview of the New Physics*, Gary Zukav points out some sublimely elegant similarities between Eastern enlightenment and the new physics. Tantra, he points out, transcends rationality just as the new physics must, as "the profound physicists of this century increasingly have become aware that they are confronting the ineffable."[12] Zukav cites Max Planck, the father of quantum mechanics: "Science . . . means unresting endeavor and continually progressing development toward an aim which the poetic intuition may apprehend, but which the intellect can never fully grasp" (Zukav, 313). That is almost identical to something Lorca, very much a mystic poet himself, said: "Through poetry man more quickly approaches the edge where the philosopher and the mathematician turn their backs in silence" (Forman and Josephs, 69). Zukav concludes that this reaching "the end of science," that is, rational science, "means the coming of western civilization . . . into the higher dimensions of human experience" (Zukav, 313).

That is precisely what I think Hemingway was reaching for in his own way more than half a century ago. Putting aside the real war and his own experience, leaving behind the observed and the observable, going beyond the rational, taking all chances, he invented his own undiscovered country. It had diverse aspects, but the greatest of these—the one he was most interested in—was love. And Hemingway knew that the way to realize love most fully and most transcendentally was by going within. As the scene in which the earth moves reveals, the true undiscovered country was the fertile, high meadow of his own imagination. There is where the dance is, and Pilar the seer is the one who reveals that transcendence through Jordan and María to us.

María and Jordan hint at it. He says: " . . . I feel as though I wanted to die when I am loving thee." And she replies, "I die each time. Do you not die?" His answer seems to make an interesting distinction between the soul's flight in ecstasy and the soul's complete release in death: "No. Almost. But did thee feel the earth move?" And she confirms it: "Yes. As I died" (160).

Between this conversation and Pilar's confirmation of their experience, Jordan experiences an extraordinary stream of consciousness that associates virtually all the novel's main themes. First he thinks of the problem of the bridge, seeing it very clearly, then worrying, and finally reminding himself not to worry. Thinking and worrying, like rational twins, are very nearly always the same. Frequently both are tied to the politics of the war. Here are Jordan's succinct thoughts on the subject:

> He was under Communist discipline for the duration of the war. Here in Spain the Communists offered the best discipline and the soundest and sanest for the prosecution of the war. He accepted their discipline for the duration of the war because, in the conduct of the war, they were the only party whose program and whose discipline he could respect.

> What were his politics then? *He had none now*, he told himself. But do not tell any one else that, he thought. Don't ever admit that. And what are you going to do afterwards? I am going back and earn my living teaching Spanish as before, and *I am going to write a true book*. (163; my emphasis)

Jordan's realpolitik may have been communism, but his real politics were the benign anarchy of the artist, exactly Ernest Hemingway's politics. Hemingway told Joe North, the editor of *New Masses*, and the members of the Lincoln Brigade that he, like Robert Jordan, "had no politics" (Bessie, 13). Jordan very realistically thinks:

> They all had the politics of horse thieves. He believed in the Republic as a form of government but the Republic would have to get rid of all of that bunch of horse thieves that brought it to the pass it was in when the rebellion started. Was there ever a people whose leaders were as truly their enemies as this one? (163)

Inevitably, inexorably, ineluctably Jordan's thinking turns to time. He wonders about the future, the future always marked by the past, even when examined humorously:

Spanish girls make wonderful wives. I've never had one so I know. And when I get my job back at the university she can be an instructor's wife and when undergraduates who take Spanish IV come in to smoke pipes in the evening and have those so valuable informal discussions about Quevedo, Lope de Vega, Galdós and the other always admirable dead, Maria can tell them about how some of the blue-shirted crusaders for the true faith sat on her head while others twisted her arms and pulled her skirts up and stuffed them in her mouth. (165)

Possibly that will not be a problem he muses, because "I suppose that I am ticketed as a Red there now for good and will be on the general blacklist" (165). In fact, Jordan might have had such a problem. Until 1 March 1964 the Abraham Lincoln Brigade was on the list of "Organizations of Security Significance" in the Armed Forces Security Questionnaire (Executive Order 10450), and whereas Jordan was not in the Lincoln Brigade, his activities in the war would surely have been subject to close scrutiny.

But time was too short for such worries. As Jordan thinks, "There is a lot of time between now and the fall term. There is a lot of time between now and day after tomorrow if you want to put it that way" (165). If he can, he will cope by writing about it, precisely again what Hemingway himself is doing: "But my guess is you will get rid of all that by writing about it, he said. Once you write it down it is all gone. It will be a good book if you can write it. Much better than the other" (165).

Probably the best passage on time in the novel occurs next. I will reproduce a certain length of it because this concern with time not only propels the action of the book but it also determines the book's meaning. It may be impossible to overstate the importance of time in *For Whom the Bell Tolls*, a subject that had concerned Hemingway profoundly at least since 1932 when in *Death in the Afternoon* he remarked, "There are some things which cannot be learned quickly and time, *which is all we have*, must be paid heavily for their acquiring" (*DIA*, 192; my emphasis). Time as the currency of life runs deeply through Jordan's thoughts:

But in the meantime all the life you have or ever will have is today, tonight, tomorrow, today, tonight, tomorrow, over and over again (I hope), he thought and so you had better take what time there is and be very thankful for it. If the bridge goes bad. It does not look too good just now.

But Maria has been good. Has she not? Oh, has she not, he thought. Maybe that is what I am to get now from life. Maybe that is my life and instead of it being threescore years and ten it is forty-eight hours or just threescore hours and ten or twelve rather. Twenty-four hours in a day would be threescore and twelve for the three full days.

I suppose it is possible to live as full a life in seventy hours as in seventy years; granted that your life has been full up to the time that the seventy hours start and that you have reached a certain age. (165–66)

Here Jordan admits to himself that he was in love with her, too, from the very first, and that he understands now what it means:

You were gone when you first saw her. When she first opened her mouth and spoke to you it was there already and you know it . . . it came the first time you looked at her as she came out bent over carrying that iron cooking platter. . . . You went strange inside every time you looked at her and every time she looked at you . . . all Pilar did was be an intelligent woman. She had taken good care of the girl and she saw what was coming the minute the girl came back into the cave with the cooking dish. (167–68)

Now Pilar becomes much more important, as she should, in Jordan's estimation, because he connects her to time and the wise use of time:

So she made things easier. She made things easier so that there was last night and this afternoon. She is a damned sight more civ-

ilized than you are and she knows what time is all about. Yes, he
said to himself, I think we can admit that she has certain notions
about the value of time. (168)

Finally Jordan comes to realize what may be "the moral of the
story," that one can only live in the present, which is all we have, and
that what counts is how we use it. Here are his ruminations, the com-
bined lessons of war and philosophy:

> I did not know that I could ever feel what I have felt, he thought.
> Nor that this could happen to me. I would like to have it for my
> whole life. You will, the other part of him said. You will. You
> have it *now* and that is all your whole life is; now. (169)

All of this is predicated upon Jordan's realization of what is happening to him, to them. Time is all any of us ever has, but in war, time
is a bit more problematical than in peace, especially if you are on a
mission behind enemy lines. War, as we know, compresses time; the
portents and bad signs only point up this compression. Love intensifies
the whole process, of course, but it also provides the only escape, in
ecstasy, and the only solution, in integration. In short, time is all we
have, but only sacred love makes profane time worthwhile. This is
Robert Jordan's simple lesson, which he characteristically turns around
and makes fun of:

> That's the thing about this sort of work, he told himself, and was
> very pleased with the thought, it isn't so much what you learn as
> it is the people you meet. He was pleased then because he was
> joking and he came back to the girl. (169)

All the themes of the novel—time, war, death, politics, and
love—receive very fine treatment in this section where Jordan's head is
now very clear, and all of them come together and make sense to
Jordan—even though he is still frequently of two minds—and to us
between the scene when the earth moves and the scene with Pilar in
which she sanctifies their ecstasy. That is not accidental. When the

earth moves, it casts a different light on everything and the mystery of love suffuses the rest of the novel.

Chapter thirteen ends with Pilar's wistful and tacit acknowledgement: "So," she says. "So there was that. So that was it" (174). And her admonition: "But do not tell it to your own people [non-Gypsies] for they will never believe you" (174). And Jordan's recognition:

> Nobody knows what tribes we came from nor what our tribal inheritance is nor what the mysteries were in the woods where the people lived that we came from. All we know is that we do not know. We know nothing about what happens to us in the nights. When it happens in the day though, it *is* something. (175)

This passage presents the dark side of our nature that so fascinated Hemingway: "tribes," "tribal inheritance," "mysteries in the woods," "nights." In a deleted passage, Pilar tells Jordan, "There is a darkness in us that you know nothing of" (Stanton, 171). That is no doubt true, as Jordan all too frequently learns. But there is a darkness in Jordan, or in Hemingway, and in all of us that Hemingway pursues here: "mysteries in the woods" can only mean the mystery religions of antiquity, the initiatory fertility cults, sometimes involving death as well as sex. As the brilliantly comprehensive thirteenth chapter closes, it snows, and the whole novel thus far seems covered in a pervasive mixture of sex, death, mystery, and snow.

As the snow falls, silently and treacherously outside, Pilar talks within the cave of her former lover, the matador Finito. Her descriptions of the bulls, the killing, the *juergas* (the flamenco parties), the unique demimonde of toreros and flamencos, including many real people such as the model for Pilar herself, Pastora Imperio, and her husband Rafael el Gallo, and the great guitarist El Niño Ricardo, and the singer La Niña de los Peines—these descriptions are also replete with sex, death and mystery. This was the primordial Spain that fascinated Hemingway. While within the Western tradition, not only Spanish but Catholic, it was also the most totally *other*, the most radically different culture Hemingway had ever experienced. All the *otherness*, all the primordiality, everything he had learned about it in eighteen years, came to bear in this novel. And his great narratrix, Pilar, tells it magnificently: "Yes. But I must tell certain details so that you will see it" (185–86). This long passage establishes Pilar as an authority in that other world, an authority that later will speak on the subject of death as though she were the pythoness of Delphi herself.

Chapter fifteen is Anselmo's. Anselmo is the Spanish conscience of the novel, always dependable but always disturbed by the need to kill human beings. He no longer prays since politics precludes it, but he misses the solace of repeated prayers. For him, "when the dark comes it is a time of great loneliness" (197). The old waiter in Hemingway's story "A Clean Well-Lighted Place," comes inevitably to mind. Anselmo impresses Jordan by staying on his post in spite of the snow: "But he stayed as he was told, Robert Jordan thought. That's the rarest thing that can happen in Spain" (200).

Back in the cave Pablo, supposedly drunk, tries to provoke Jordan by asking him what the Scotsman wears under his kilt, implying that Jordan is effeminate. Then he claims that Jordan is a false professor because he has no beard. Pablo claims to be drunk, which Jordan doubts: "Cowardly, yes" (211), he thinks. Then Jordan calls him shameless and an outright coward out loud in Spanish. Agustín, also provoked, hits Pablo twice, and Jordan prepares again to kill him. Agustín calls Pablo, "*Cabrón*" (214), a cuckold (literally a big goat), the worst insult possible in Spanish. But Pablo is oddly, shrewdly, dangerously unperturbed: "I am far past words" (214). But he is not. As he leaves the cave to see about his horses, he drops his bomb: "Where will you take them, *Inglés*, after the bridge? Where will you take the patriots? I have thought of it all day while I have been drinking" (215). Finally he remarks:

> "I have thought you are a group of illusioned people," Pablo said. "Led by a woman with her brains between her thighs and a foreigner who comes to destroy you." (215)

As he departs, he calls back, referring to the snow: "It's still falling, *Inglés*" (216).

As chapter seventeen opens, Robert Jordan resolves to kill Pablo, if necessary, but Pablo, ever shrewd, obviates that need and makes it clear that only he can lead the band to the safety of the Gredos Mountains in the west. Chapter eighteen is the chapter of the wheel with which we began. As Jordan muses about that wheel and Pablo, we understand that, as Carlos Baker had remarked, "the turning wheels may be as small as the arguments with Pablo . . . " (Baker 1972, 263). The larger wheel of three days and three nights contains many such smaller wheels, all the intricate and spun out small wheels—the narrations within the narration—that turn as the large wheel rises and falls. Here on the wheel with Jordan we are halfway through the main action, halfway through the novel. We are at the top of the larger wheel and we are about to start down, but as we begin that rapid descent, Hemingway has some circles of his own to spin out.

The first is the flashback to Gaylord's in Madrid, the wheel that reaches back through time and space to encompass the real war—to tie Hemingway's invented circles to the largest circle of all, the war itself, and the impending world struggle beyond—and to review the lessons Hemingway himself had learned. As Jordan expresses it, " . . . Gaylord's was the place you needed to complete your education" (230).

Chapter eighteen is the chapter in which a no-longer-engaged Hemingway uses his recently also no-longer-engaged character to denounce the falsehoods and the evils of the communist leadership as he, Hemingway, had seen them. Jordan arrives at that denunciation as a remembrance of nights past, allowing Hemingway to make his points about the Spanish peasant commanders who spoke Russian, such as Enrique Lister and Juan Modesto; about the ineptitude of Republican leaders, such as "the old bald, spectacled, conceited, stupid-as-an-owl, unintelligent-in-conversation, brave-and-as-dumb-as-a-bull, propaganda-built-up defender of Madrid, Miaja;" or about the Internationals, such as "Gall, the Hungarian, who ought to be shot if you could believe half you heard at Gaylord's" (233).

Perhaps more important we get a chance to understand Jordan's early belief in the cause and his faith in it. Contrasted to the decadence at Gaylord's, he remembers the "puritanical, religious communism of Velazquez 63, the Madrid palace that had been turned into the International Brigade headquarters in the capital. At Velazquez 63 it was like being a member of a religious order . . . " (234–35).

For Jordan these early experiences were like "taking part in a crusade" (235). We must look at his early feelings in the war here, for they show us a dedicated Jordan, one whose former dedication contrasts revealingly with his later more cynical or realistic attitude:

> You felt, in spite of all bureaucracy and inefficiency and party strife something that was like the feeling you expected to have and did not have when you made your first communion. It was a feeling of consecration to a duty toward all of the oppressed of the world which would be as difficult and embarrassing to speak about as religious experience and yet it was authentic as the feeling you had when you heard Bach, or stood in Chartres Cathedral or the Cathedral at León and saw the light coming through the great windows; or when you saw Mantegna and Greco and Brueghel in the Prado. It gave you a part in something that you could believe in wholly and completely and in which you felt an absolute brotherhood with the others. . . . (235)

"Religious order," "crusade," "first communion," "consecration," "religious experience," "Chartres Cathedral," "the Cathedral at León": Hemingway makes it pretty plain how Jordan *had* felt. You do not have to be a deconstructionist to figure out what the message is. Over and again, the Republic's (i.e., the communists') abolition of religion notwithstanding (or *especially* notwithstanding), Hemingway employs religious imagery and the language of religion, sometimes in an orthodox fashion, sometimes mystically, to describe the most important emotions in the novel, including by contrast Jordan's disillusionment:

> So you fought, he thought. And in the fighting soon there was no purity of feeling for those who survived the fighting and were good at it. Not after the first six months. (235)

Despite all the longstanding misguided critics of Hemingway, if we look at the texts of his works, we cannot fail to be impressed with the spiritual nature of his fictional quest, and nowhere is that spiritual quality more evident than in *For Whom the Bell Tolls*. Even though Jordan loses his early political idealism, later on he is forced into admitting the existence of mystical rapture, la gloria:

> I am no mystic, but to deny it [la gloria] is as ignorant as though you denied the telephone or that the earth revolves around the sun or that there are other planets than this. (380)

Perhaps Jordan would agree with Pilar, who states early in the novel with her characteristic irony: "There probably still is God after all, although we have abolished Him" (88). Pilar's best proof of God, ironically, is María's lack of venereal disease in spite of having been raped repeatedly.

Chapter eighteen also allows us a glimpse of the early fighting Jordan participated in: in the first battles of the war in the Guadarramas in the summer of 1936; in the house-to-house fighting in the fall at Usera and Carabanchel, the southwestern suburbs of Madrid where the capital was "saved" at least temporarily; and at Pozoblanco on the Córdoba front in Andalucía. Of those early days Jordan thinks, "You were in a sort of state of grace" (237).

It is interesting that Hemingway places Jordan in the province of Córdoba and has him think, "You could remember the men you knew who died in the fighting around Pozoblanco; but it was a joke at Gaylord's" (239). A Russian guerrilla named Starinov operated in that sector and successfully blew up a troop train full of Italian troops. And an American named Irving Goff, one of the very few Americans who in fact operated behind the lines, who carried a submachine gun and hid in a cave, also helped blow up another train full of Italians. Later on Goff blew up other trains as well as a bridge (Wyden, 314–18). In many ways Irving Goff's story was much closer to Jordan's than his supposed model, Major Robert Merriman.

Chapter nineteen, which brings us almost to the end of Day Two, is the famous "smell of death" chapter. Hemingway knew he was pushing his reader's credibility in this chapter. He told Faulkner that here he was taking chances and parenthetically that the smell of death was "no shit" (*Letters*, 624). Somewhat more formally he maintained to Charles Scribner that it was "an integral and valid part" of the novel:

> There is the balancing of Jordan's good sense and sound skepticism against this gypsy crap which isn't all crap. And to make the gypsy thing valid and not just seeming phony as all that stuff always does I needed some completely *naturalistic* thing which gives some of the *horror* that is in Madrid. (*Letters*, 508; my emphasis)

He wrote Maxwell Perkins that unless it would impair the sale of the book, the chapter should be left in:

> The passage is meant to be horrifying. It is not meant to be gratuitously obscene or unpublishable. But I have to somehow give that quality of Madrid and make the idea of the odour earthily and concretely and vulgarly believable—instead of seeming to be gypsy-cross-my-hand-with-silver-nonsense. Real gypsies are a very strange people and the ones in this book are not book-gypsies anymore than my indians were ever book-indians. (*Letters*, 513)

Hemingway refers to this passage about the smell of death, then, as "no shit," "not phoney," "[not] crap," and "not book-gypsies." Why is Hemingway being defensive? There are two reasons, I believe. First, very few people in the U.S., especially then, were comfortable talking about death, particularly something as horrible as the stench of death. Our culture is and has been a culture that avoids death, avoids talking about it, avoids dealing with it, and avoids accepting it as the natural consequence of life. Spain on the other hand is, from our point of view, a culture that is extremely, even morbidly, death-centered. Hemingway knew that, understood it, found it profoundly important as well as entirely appropriate to his material, and made it one of his most important subjects.

Second, Hemingway is dealing here with the purely intuitive. This subject is not rational, and Jordan, who is very rational, has trouble accepting Pilar's statements. Even Pablo does not believe it altogether. So Hemingway is faced with getting us to believe something his own characters doubt. At the same time Hemingway insisted on its veracity to his editor and to his publisher. The scene itself is, of course, invented, but the allusions in it are not totally fabricated, as we will see.

Pilar maintains that she could *see* death on Kashkin. "I saw death there as plainly as though it were sitting on his shoulder" (251), she says, echoing something Hemingway told Scribner, " . . . haveing seen people walking around with it sitting on their shoulders . . . " (*Letters*, 508). Is this contagion or was Hemingway drawing from actual personal experience? There is probably no way to know, although we do know that Hemingway later mentioned the smell of death on at least two occasions during World War II, once accurately predicting the death of a major (Baker 1969, 407, 434). At any rate it is well known that some Gypsies have rather remarkable intuitive powers, possibly due to the fact that they do not spend their lives trapping themselves in left-brained consciousness but remain more open to intuitive or right-brained awareness than we do (and also, of course, to fears, superstition, etc.).

When Pilar uses examples, she picks real people, not fictional characters. She explains how Blanquet could smell death on Granero and on Joselito and how many could smell it on Ignacio Sánchez Mejías. All three of them were real toreros who were killed in the ring, and Blanquet was a real *banderillero*, too, so those deaths were historical and not made up at all. (In fact all the details about the toreros are historically accurate. Only Pilar and Finito are fictional.)

Joselito was the brother of Rafael el Gallo who, as we have seen, was married to Pastora Imperio, Pilar's model. José's and Rafael's sister, Dolores, married the valiant Ignacio Sánchez Mejías, whose death in the arena was the subject of Lorca's great "Lament." The niece of all three, Rafael, José, and Dolores (the daughter of their sister Gabriela) is the famous flamenco reciter, Gabriela Ortega (her father was an Ortega). In other words, we are back in the center of the most famous flamenco-torero clan of Spanish Gypsies of all time. Gabriela the reciter recounted in May 1988 on Jesús Quintero's television program *El perro verde*, an interesting story related to the death of her famous uncle, Joselito, in the *plaza de toros* of Talavera de la Reina on 16 May 1920. She was a little girl in Sevilla at the time, and the night before the goring she dreamed about his death, waking up screaming: "¡A mi tío se lo comen las moscas, a mi tío se lo comen las moscas! (The flies are eating my uncle, the flies are eating my uncle!)" The next evening the telegram arrived bearing the news that put all of Spain into mourning.

Does that prove anything about the smell of death? No; but it does show how stories—then and now—about these famous artists become well known and how they naturally involve such topics as death and premonitions or precognitions. When I heard Gabriela telling the story, I could not help associating it with Pilar's claims.

The smell of death, according to Pilar, is a wretched mixture of natural odors: brass when you are seasick, the breath of old women who drink bull's blood at the slaughterhouse, rotting flowers, earth, and the "odor of love's labor lost mixed sweetly with soapy water and cigarette butts" (256). It is disgusting, and we understand why Jordan does not want to smell it. But where did Hemingway get his inspiration? What experience did he use to invent it? I can not answer that in full, but I can answer part of it.

The smells of love's labor, the earth, and the rotting flowers are all logical enough; mixed together they form what Pilar calls "the smell that is both the death and birth of man" (256). The odor that seems most offensive is the breath of "the old women who go before daylight to drink the blood of the beasts that are slaughtered." Such an old woman Jordan should kiss as she emerges from the slaughterhouse,

> with her face gray and her eyes hollow, and the whiskers of age
> on her chin, and on her cheeks, set in the waxen white of her face
> as the sprouts grow from the seed of a bean, not bristles, but pale
> sprouts in the death of her face. . . . (255)

This description bothers even the Gypsy, Rafael—" That of the sprouts in the face of the old women sickens me" (255)—yet it is all based in reality. Pilar embellishes the business of the sprouts, but the drinking of the blood at the slaughterhouse is no invention. The Spanish painter and writer José Gutiérrez Solana has described how in the twenties tubercular patients came to the Madrid slaughterhouse to drink bull's blood as a cure. And another writer, Eugenio Noel, has confirmed this practice.[13]

Hemingway doubtless heard the same sort of thing, possibly when he was researching *Death in the Afternoon*, and he may have saved it for when he needed it. At any rate the association of bull's blood and magical cures is well documented from antiquity forward, especially in such mystery religions as Mithraism and the cult of Cybele, which celebrated a rite called the *taurobolium* that involved baptism in a sacrificed bull's blood. And Gerald Brenan tells of the case of a Gypsy called La Leona, the lioness, who was found in the mountains south of Granada drinking the blood of human babies to cure her consumption (Brenan, 177).

I am not trying to take the mystery away from this passage; on the contrary I am trying to show that Hemingway was concerned with rooting the mystery in actual physical reality. He was, in fact, very concerned with that physical reality because under no circumstances did he want Pilar to be considered a phony or a "book-gypsy." Certain Spanish Gypsies, especially those of the Ortega and related clans (not to be confused with La Leona) are indeed extraordinary people, and Hemingway wanted to make sure that their intuitive brilliance, not some Gypsy stereotype, shone through. Otherwise the mystery of death here would be simply claptrap. And if that mystery is claptrap, then all the others are as well, and the novel collapses like a house of tarot cards.

Hemingway was, I believe, operating from real phenomena he had experienced or heard of and in the existence of which he surely believed. (As the case of La Leona illustrates, there were many unusual practices still taking place in Spain at that time). There is a dark side to Hemingway that critics have yet to explore much, including androgyny, alchemy, reincarnation, all the "mysteries," in fact, associated with the intuitive or imaginative part of human experience, all those thresholds and subliminalities crossed frequently by creative artists. In any case, the interconnectedness of birth, death, and sex is as obvious as anything in life. The aspect that is difficult for us to deal with is the idea that death can be "smelled," or somehow sensed ahead. I wish I could agree with Rafael that the smell of death "is a well-known thing among us [the Gypsies]" (254), but I have found no evidence to support that contention. I have talked with a number of Andalusian Gypsies about it and never had it confirmed (nor denied, for that matter), but many of their customs and beliefs have been lost. And, too, Gypsies are not exactly given to a discussion of these things.

Carol Zaleski, in her fascinating study *Otherworld Journeys: Accounts of Near-death Experience in Medieval and Modern Times*, reminds us that *Homo sapiens* (which means literally, man tasting or smelling, and by extension wise man) is "as the world's scriptures tell us, a creature familiar with the taste of death." She cites as evidence an example from the Koran (Sura 21:35): "Every soul shall taste of death;" and from Psalms 89:48: "What man can live and never see death?"[14]

"Taste" death, "see" death; but "smell" death? Colin Wilson, the noted and prolific English writer on the criminal, the occult, and the supernatural, cites this description by Rosalind Heywood, a mildly clairvoyant housewife who had several alleged experiences with the previously deceased:

> As I hurried into his room [Vivian's, her friend who had died ten days before] to fetch the picture I was shocked by a sickening blast of what I have come to call the smell of death. I am never quite sure whether this is physical or what a sensitive would call borderline. . . .[15]

My point is not about such cases at all, but simply that at least one person, totally unconnected to our endeavor here, reports the "smell of death," as a sensation which is not necessarily physical, but perhaps borderline, which is to say only perceivable to someone who is open to such a reading of reality. As Pilar tells Jordan, "It is not that thou art stupid. Thou art simply deaf. One who is deaf cannot hear music." She goes on to remark that she saw Kashkin's death "as though it were burned there with an iron." And she smelled it: "And what is more he smelt of death." Her descriptions, mixing the senses, are all metaphoric, " . . . as plainly *as though* it were sitting on his shoulder" (251; my emphasis). Her reading of reality is clearly psychical rather than physical.

Carol Zaleski wonders if, in fact, our ability to "taste death" is not what makes us wise:

> We know that we will die, and that knowledge invades our consciousness, shapes our artifacts, *arts*, and sciences; it will not let us rest until we have found ways, through rituals and *stories*, theologies and philosophies, either to make sense of death or, failing that, to make sense of ourselves in the face of death. (Zaleski, 12; my emphasis)

That is a wonderful description of what Hemingway was doing with the smell of death passage and by extension with his whole career as a writer. As Zaleski also remarks, death "galvanizes the imagination" (Zaleski, 12). It certainly galvanized Hemingway's, a fact we will come back to in the concluding chapter, but it galvanized it into inventing, as usual, from what he actually knew. When Pilar "smells" the death of Kashkin she may well be "encountering an aspect of human personality that is at present unknown to science," as Colin Wilson expresses the faculty, which is to say unknown to the rational mind. She was perhaps, again to use Wilson's words, "demonstrating that the unconscious mind has access to 'hidden' information" (Wilson 1985, 255). That is precisely what I think Hemingway was alluding to when he told Maxwell Perkins, "Real gypsies are a very strange people . . . " (*Letters*, 513). We have already called Pilar seer and shaman, which means that she has a privileged access to the intuitive, to the right brain, perhaps even to the unconscious mind. As such, she understands both the ecstasy of la gloria and the mystery of death far better than most of us.

In the next chapter (twenty), as Day Two comes to a close, Jordan counters in his own mind with smells of life. María comes barefoot through the snow to the sleeping robe and tells Jordan "I love thee . . . and I am thy wife" (262).

María voices the sense of completeness, of unity that they now share:

> "Afterwards we will be as one animal of the forest and be so close that neither one can tell that one of us is one and not the other. Can you not feel my heart be your heart? . . . I am thee and thou art me and all of one is the other. . . . I would have us exactly the same. . . . But we will be one now and there will never be a separate one. I will be thee *when thou art not there.*" (262–63; my emphasis)

This is the language of ecstasy, the expression of union, the recapitulation in words of their physical sexuality, but the last sentence also foreshadows exactly what will happen at the end of the novel.

Jordan tells María: "And I love thee and I love thy name, María" (263), pointing out through her name the clearly spiritual way he feels about this woman whose name is María, who is "thy wife," and "an animal of the forest." They sleep "making an alliance against death," but Jordan wakes and holds her "as though she were all of life and it was being taken from him." And then he lies there in the dark, toward the end of the second night, "thinking" (264).

12

The Action: Day Three

The second "half" of the novel is shorter, and it contains more action with fewer digressions or small circles than the first half, consequently requiring less explanation. It begins at dawn when Jordan, from his sleeping robe, kills the Navarrese cavalryman and the band prepares for a possible assault. The rising tension is broken only by Rafael's killing of the hares mating in the snow, comical because of his description—"You cannot imagine what a debauch they were engaged in" (274)—but not a particularly good omen for the lovers Robert and María, also trapped in the snow.

The band's luck holds for now, and the enemy cavalry passes by, following the wily Pablo's tracks away from the camp. After it is over Jordan reflects on Agustín's desire to kill:

> Yes, Robert Jordan thought. We do it coldly but they do not, nor ever have. It is their extra sacrament. Their old one that they had before the new religion came from the far end of the Mediterranean, the one they have never abandoned but only suppressed and hidden to bring it out again in wars and inquisitions. They are the people of the Auto de Fé; the act of faith. (286)

The Action: Day Three

Typically then Jordan reverses himself and admits that he too has been "corrupted" by killing, and that he felt excitement "At every train." Also he respects Anselmo who does not like the killing of men: "He is a Christian. Something very rare in Catholic countries" (287). Jordan is, of course, being ironic here, as he was about the "Auto de Fé," which was the Inquisition's euphemism for burning supposed heretics at the stake.

As much as Jordan loves Spain—as much as Hemingway does—he is not tempted to idealize its history. Jordan/Hemingway are making a reasoned judgment here, and it is not one made lightly. Hemingway loved Spain better than any place, at least during certain periods of his life, but he did not see it through rose-colored glasses. On the contrary he understood that Spain's genius and its devil were like two Janus-faces of the same being. As he wrote to art critic Bernard Berenson from Cuba much later, "You know that what ruined, and what made Spain, was the Inquisition . . . " (*Letters*, 812).

After the danger is gone, Jordan and Agustín have breakfast (Jordan like Hemingway eats onions) and discuss María. Agustín tells Jordan that Pilar had guarded her fiercely from the men, and so he does not understand why she has given María to Jordan "as a present" (290). Jordan explains that afterward María will go with him and that they will be married. Agustín reminds Jordan that under the revolution it would not be necessary to marry, but, he adds, with characteristic respect for tradition, "it would be better" (291).

Agustín is also much taken with María, and he is careful to explain her conduct to Jordan: "You do not understand how such a girl would be if there had been no revolution." When Arturo Barea objected strenuously to María's forwardness as unrealistic, he seemed not to have taken this discussion into account. Hemingway is clearly conscious of her unusual behavior, and he takes pains to justify it. As Jordan explains to Agustín, "It is because of the lack of time that there has been informality. What we do not have is time. . . . We must live all of our life in this time" (291–92). Strict realism and strict behavior must give way to the horological imperative, which may not be sociologically correct under normal conditions but, as Hemingway takes pains to make clear, in wartime certainly occurs.

The incident with the cavalry, given Jordan's cool command, has earned him greater trust with Agustín, who now begins a review of all the members of the band for Jordan's benefit. All are fit except for "two weak elements: the gypsy and Pablo. But the band of Sordo are as much better than we are as we are better than goat manure" (293). Just then Jordan hears, faintly at first, then distinctly, "the precise, crackling, curling roll of automatic rifle fire" (293), and he realizes that El Sordo's camp has been attacked. Agustín wants to help them, but Jordan explains to him that help is impossible and that they must remain where they are for the sake of the mission.

El Sordo had stolen horses—horses that Robert Jordan and the band sorely need—the night before and, as Jordan reasons, "The snow stopped and they tracked them up there." Jordan understands they have no chance: "They were lost when the snow stopped" (296). Just as the mating hares were betrayed by their tracks in the new fallen snow, so El Sordo's band was doomed too. Jordan will lose the horses and his best allies. As if to seal Sordo's fate, the observation plane comes by, "the bad luck bird" (299), as Pilar remarks, which will send the attack planes to bomb El Sordo's band into oblivion.

At this point Robert Jordan, frequently of two minds, has a serious talk with himself, reviewing his ideas on killing, on politics, and on his love for María. Here is the passage on love:

> And another thing. Don't ever kid yourself about loving some one. It is just that most people are not lucky enough ever to have it. What you have with Maria, whether it lasts just through today and a part of tomorrow, or whether it lasts for a long life is the most important thing that can happen to a human being. There will always be people who say it does not exist because they cannot have it. But I tell you it is true and that you have it and that you are lucky even if you die tomorrow. (305)

Basically Jordan is reiterating what we already know. His politics are American, slightly anarchistic, and decidedly non-dialectical and non-materialistic, especially now that he has María. His love for María has certainly displaced any Marxist notions he once might have harbored.

The Action: Day Three

Love has become his religion: "most people are not lucky enough ever to have it"; "the most important thing that can happen to a human being." There is nothing new, but the passage is worth noting because Hemingway makes a point of telling it all again. Hemingway has Jordan give himself some pretty sound advice, but as he is thinking about how he has gotten El Sordo "into a fine jam" (305), he hears "the far-off, distant throbbing and, looking up, he saw the planes" (306).

El Sordo's fight from the hilltop, his last stand in chapter twenty-seven, is one of the most celebrated pieces of Hemingway's action writing. Hemingway himself liked it enough to include it in the war anthology he edited, *Men at War*. We have already seen how Hemingway's irony carved up specious propaganda, especially when young Joaquín tries to remember La Pasionaria's slogans but is unable to remember anything but his prayers to the Virgin; and we have seen how at the fateful moment, the earth moves in death when it drops from the "mechanized doom" of the planes. And finally, we have already met El Sordo, one of Hemingway's best drawn minor figures (whose characterization even Arturo Barea commends). Stanton writes insightfully that "El Sordo resembles one of those popular heroes who fought against the French in the Spanish War of Independence depicted in Goya's *Disasters [of War]*" (Stanton, 179). In this war from 1808–1814, the Spanish fought against Napoleon's troops in skirmishes or *guerrillas* (little wars), whence the term guerrilla warfare. Guerrilla warfare is as old as the Iberian tribes that gave the Roman legions so much trouble, but the term derives from the Napoleonic period.

El Sordo is the essential guerrilla warrior who seems to have sprung fully formed from Hemingway's imagination. He is particularly important because he is the embodiment of a kind of Spaniard who was being eradicated, the primitive, loyal, brave man of the soil that modern warfare had no place for. Allen Guttman has understood Hemingway's primitivism well, and what he says is appropriate to El Sordo:

> Confronted by the mechanized enemy, Hemingway's primitivism
> becomes an impossible vision, but that is *not* to say that the values

associated with primitivism are not still valid ones; one need not be a primitivist to feel that technological society today is both repressive and frighteningly unstable.[1]

When we watch El Sordo's heroic defense of his hill, we cannot help agreeing and hating the planes that destroy him.

Perhaps most poetic and most suitable of all is Teunissen's vision of the guerrillas as very much like American Indians, especially El Sordo:

> One cannot resist drawing attention . . . to the character and fate of El Sordo, "a man of few words" with "a thin-bridged, hooked nose like an Indian's," who speaks Tontoese prose—"when blow bridge?"—who drinks not wine but firewater, and who dies on top of a hill outnumbered and outgunned, sheltered at last behind the body of his dead horse (pp. 140, 141, 198, 307ff). (Teunissen, 230)

Jordan frequently thinks of Indians and of the American Civil War, so the analogy is most appropriate. Hemingway did not make book-Gypsies, book-Indians or book-guerrillas because he understood them all, including their similarities, as independent peoples still living within nature. The bell tolls for all of us, but most especially it tolls for Hemingway's natural people, his Indians, his Gypsies, his Sordos, and beyond them for all the fishing Santiagos plying the deep waters of the world in small boats.

One other character, whose sympathetic portrayal drew fire from the Left, emerges from El Sordo's last stand—but on the other side—the Nationalist Lieutenant Paco Berrendo. Contrasted with the fatal insanity of his superior, Captain Mora, Lt. Berrendo's appealing equanimity is noticeable, even as he must order the guerrillas' heads taken for identification. Hemingway did his level best to keep things from being black and white. Ironically, *berrendo* means two-colored and is applied especially to bulls, the most common color being red and white (as in extreme Left and extreme Right) and black and white. And his positioning of Berrendo, the good Nationalist from Navarre,

Hemingway's favorite Spanish region, in Jordan's sights at the novel's end, is as intentional as it is poignant.

Chapter twenty-eight opens with the eating of the stewed hares the Gypsy had killed, but the silence from El Sordo's direction hangs over the meal like a pall. Lt. Berrendo marches on toward La Granja, entering the forest with "the light coming through the tree trunks in patches as it comes through the columns of a cathedral" (326). He is praying for his dead friend. Old Anselmo, counting bodies dead and alive, watches them ride past. Coming back, he finds the headless bodies on the hill, and returns to camp, praying now for the first time since the war had begun and feeling comforted by the prayers.

In chapter twenty-nine, the novel splits into several simultaneous actions. This splitting technique was well known to conventional novelists because it could heighten interest and create suspense. (Edgar Rice Burroughs, whom Hemingway read enthusiastically as a boy, used it extensively.) In Hemingway's case, however, it is unusual, as his normal tendency was to follow one action through from beginning to end. Also, while it is effective for action, it is somewhat arbitrary and does not enhance the elegant wheel-like movement we have followed up to this point. Yet it was evidently necessary for the progression of the plot.

Jordan picks Andrés, who is dependable and younger than Anselmo, to take a message through the lines to General Golz to try to persuade him to have the attack canceled due to the anticipatory Nationalist troop movement setting up to foil the offensive. While Andrés travels, Jordan remembers his father's suicide, remembers how he got rid of the gun by dropping it into the deep lake, and remembers his grandfather who was a Civil War hero and Jordan's own hero as well. He condemns his father as a coward and recalls how his father was driven to suicide by his mother's bullying, autobiographical aspects Hemingway transferred to Jordan. Hemingway makes good use of them, however, for Jordan will have to consider suicide at the end of the novel, a suicide that has been hanging over him since the first mention of death-smelling Kashkin in chapter two. Jordan concludes, as usual, that thinking is not such a good idea, not unless he can think about the Republic taking La Granja by the following night. Consistently in *For Whom the Bell Tolls*, thinking portends death.

Chapter thirty-one, in the sleeping robe, does not bode well either. María has "a great soreness and much pain," and they are unable to make love: " . . . it was not good luck for the last night" (341). Instead they talk and dream of being together in Madrid, an escape that appeals to María because Pilar had told her that "we would all die tomorrow" (345). In their fantasy they speak of having hair the same length and of looking alike, a very normal desire in young lovers, not at all the fetish or the narcissism that some biographers have claimed, but the language and desire of passion and unity.

María also tells her story, the account of the shooting of her mother and father, the shaving of her head, and her treatment up to but not including her being raped. Her descriptions are a kind of counter to Pilar's tale of the massacre, not as long or detailed but with splendid images such as the following that seems taken straight from Picasso's most violent cubist portraits. As María has her head shaved, she watches in the mirror:

> . . . I cried and I cried but I could not look away from the horror that my face made with the mouth open and the braids tied in it and my head coming naked under the clippers. (352)

As the chapter ends Jordan sanctifies their union: "We are married, now. I marry thee now. Thou art my wife" (354). And then he thinks, hating, then forgiving:

> Those who did that [to María] are the last flowering of what their education has produced. Those are the flowers of Spanish chivalry. What a people they have been. What sons of bitches from Cortez, Pizarro, Menéndez de Avila all down through Enrique Lister to Pablo. And what wonderful people. There is no finer and no worse people in the world. No kinder and no crueler. (354–55)

More philosophically he muses, bringing us once again to the central facts of the matter, "Maybe I have had all my life in three days" (355).

Then as María sleeps, he whispers in English very quietly, "I'd like to marry you, rabbit. I'm very proud of your family" (355).

After Chapter thirty-two, in which we switch to Gaylord's in Madrid in order to overhear the false report that the fascists have been bombing their own troops, Pablo deserts, taking with him the exploder, the detonators, the fuse, and the caps. At this point, Jordan has the following lined up against him: the Republic has a false notion of the state of the enemy; the enemy is aware of and moving against the offensive; the horses and allies of El Sordo's band are no more; and now Jordan has lost Pablo and some of the necessary equipment to blow the bridge. The only thing that can save him is Andrés going with the message.

Andrés, called the Bulldog of Villaconejos in his home pueblo (which means Rabbit Village, and, yes, there is such a village, not far to the south of the Arganda Bridge), crosses the lines with his message for Golz. As he goes he remembers the *capeas*, the village bullbaiting in the square during the town's fiesta. Through Andrés's reminiscence Hemingway provides us with another indelible sketch of Spanish life before the war, that rural Mediterranean life which stretched back unbroken for centuries into a remote past so utterly different from our own world, that timeless world coming quickly to an end in the mechanized doom of the war. Andrés is happy with his thoughts of rural life until he comes to the "government position where he knew he would be challenged" (368).

Jordan, in the sleeping robe, continues to think and to blame himself for Pablo's treachery and to damn Spaniards in general. He damns them all always and forever in his violent raging temper, coming only momentarily to one instant of piety. Amid all the various euphemistic "muckings," he thinks, "God pity the Spanish people. Any leader they have will muck them" (370). When his rage finally abates and he figures out what he will do, he thinks, "We'll be killed but we'll blow the bridge." And then he lies there, holding María, "feeling her breathe and feeling her heart beat, and keeping track of the *time* on his wrist watch" (371; my emphasis).

Andrés runs into some trouble when he gets to the Republican zone. He is allowed to cross in but is delayed by the stupidity and the moronic behavior of the slovenly anarchist types at the crossing, people Andrés thinks are "like dangerous children; dirty, foul, undisciplined, kind, loving, silly and ignorant but always dangerous because they were armed" (377).

Meanwhile Jordan is watching "time passing on his wrist. It went slowly, almost imperceptibly, for it was a small watch and he could not see the second hand. But as he watched the minute hand he found he could almost check its motion with his concentration" (378). Chapter thirty-seven is the most time-obsessed chapter in this completely time-obsessed novel. Jordan, almost believing (wishfully thinking) his rational faculties can halt the movement of time, sees "where the lance-pointed, luminous splinter moved slowly up the left face of the dial." Then, "He could see the hand moving on the watch," and shortly "he saw the hand of the watch now mounting in sharp angle toward the top where the hour was" (378).

María wakes, miraculously now with no pain, and the love scene that follows is the ultimate abolition of time in fiction that I know of. All the words concentrate into a continuous present, crowd into an eternal now, seemingly stopping the fatal march of time again, not now so much physically within space-time as rhetorically through word-time, merging two into one in the timelessness of *now*. Observe in the passage the recurrence of "now" and "one," all the "nows" and the "ones" composing and comprising la gloria. You may think la gloria is as mythical as Socrates' once perfect male-and-female-being reconstituted, but it is the living myth—and the peak-experience—that lovers in ecstasy actually perceive. If we do not experience it literally ourselves, we can at least experience it vicariously, as Pilar in her wisdom did when the earth moved. Or, just as we may not experience San Juan de la Cruz's religious mysticism literally, yet vicariously, through his poetry, we can share his sublime rapture. What Hemingway has attempted here is indeed ambitious, so much so that it is worthy of our total concentration to try to understand the mystery within the poetry. The passage opens softly, then begins to build:

> Then they were together so that as the hand on the watch moved, unseen now, they knew that nothing could ever happen to the one

that did not happen to the other, that no other thing could happen more than this; that this was all and always; this was what had been and now and whatever was to come. This, that they were not to have, they were having.

Then almost suddenly, almost fiercely, the intensity of the words and of the rhythm increases and the religious allusions begin:

They were having now and before and always and now and now and now. Oh, now, now, now, the only now, and above all now, and there is no other now but thou now and now is thy prophet. Now and forever now. Come now, now, for there is no now but now. Yes, now. Now, please now, only now, not anything else only this now, and where are you and where am I and where is the other one, and not why, not ever why, only this now; and on and always please then always now, always now, for now always one now; one only one, there is no other one but one now, one, going now, rising now, sailing now, leaving now, wheeling now, soaring now, away now, all the way now, all of all the way now; one and one is one, is one, is one, is one, is still one, is still one, is one descendingly, is one softly, is one longingly, is one kindly, is one happily, is one in goodness, is one to cherish, is one now on earth with elbows against the cut and slept-on branches of the pine tree with the smell of the pine boughs and the night; to earth conclusively now, and with the morning of the day to come. (379)

"One and one is one": the negation of all logic, of all rationality, the sublime and fearless surrender of self into the other, of the I in the thou. As Jordan says, "No one is there alone" (380). This is what he has learned:

How little we know of what there is to know. I wish that I were going to live a long time instead of going to die today because I have learned much about life in these four days; more I think than in all the other time. . . . I wish there was more time. (380)

At the center of what he has learned is the mystery of la gloria, that seeming timelessness that encompasses all time: "They were having now and before and always"; and yet that is so inexorably bracketed by time: "the watch moved, unseen now . . . with the morning of the day to come" (379). In the original manuscript version of this passage, Hemingway revealed some of his intention, writing that this was their reward and that "only by giving can it be received" (KL:EH 83, 36–5. In Hemingway's unusual numbering system, 36–5 means chapter thirty-six, page 5). In another deleted sentence Jordan felt "happy with an ecstasy of fulfillment" (KL:EH 83, 36–5). There is nothing new about these ideas, but their expression in a prose style charged through and through with religious imagery and allusions, one that imitates verbally the act of love, rather than simply describing it, is not only new but, I would venture, as the language of ecstasy, has not been matched in prose.

" . . . and where are you and where am I and where is the other one, and not why, not ever why, only this now . . . " Any sense of "why," of the nagging rational, is overcome by this all encompassing *now*, and all sense of self, of two separate beings, is annihilated. Long before modern psychologists began to popularize such ideas, Hemingway understood perfectly that the animus and the anima, the male in the female and the female in the male, could only find each other and complement each other if the normally impregnable barriers of rationality and the ego were let down.

The essence of this ecstasy is loss of self and unity, the latter impossible without the former. "Where are you and where am I" is a perfect expression of the loss of self. "Where is the other one": to see *otherness* is the essence of selfhood, of the ego. In ecstasy the walls of Jericho of the ego come tumbling down, permitting the merger of two into one. If there is no *other*, there is only one: "One and one is one." The ego withers, the self dissolves, the two are made one, selfless, timeless, transported, fused, and enraptured in la gloria.

Romantic? In our society yes, the stuff of celluloid dreams, but for believers in the mystical oneness of all things, for initiates in mysticism, erotic transport is only one of the surest paths to bliss. This is true for Hindus and Buddhists; for the Gnostics, including the Gnostic Jesus; for the medieval troubadours singing the praises of courtly love; for the writers of the medieval Jewish *Cabala* of Spain that influenced

San Juan de la Cruz and many other mystics; in the modern psychology of C. G. Jung and his legion of followers; and in Hemingway, John Donne (read his poem "The Ecstasy" in which two lovers fuse their souls into one), Shakespeare, Petrarch, and Goethe, to name a few of the best (and all poets, notice, except Hemingway, who really is as well); not to mention for all the believers in the ancient mystery religions rooted in shamanism and celebrating the paired sky-fathers and earth-mothers that once spread across the known world from India to Spain. If I risk overstating the case, it is because I believe that Hemingway was seeking nothing less than the once-perfect being, the male and female halves indeed reunited, the *homo totus* of Greek myth and modern psychology and myriad religions, the coincidence of opposites that takes us closer to harmony and perfection than any other human endeavor. Hemingway's ideal was not mere romance; it was a perfect example of one of the most consistently compelling visions in human discourse since the inception of discourse itself, or if you prefer, since the inception of religion, art, and psychology, especially if we take the latter literally to mean the logos (the discourse) of the psyche (the soul).

Biographer Kenneth Lynn's notion that Robert and María's merging is due to "Hemingway's peculiar childhood"[2] is sadly typical of the muddling the psycho-biographers engage in, and typical, too, of the lack of understanding in our Western culture of the nature of passion, ecstasy, and rapture. To attribute Hemingway's quest for ecstasy to a childhood aberration is to miss altogether his gifted insights into the psychology of love, the physiology of love, and especially the language of love.

This language of love had been a part of Hemingway's life for a long time. Gioia Diliberto, the latest biographer of Hadley Richardson, writes that Hadley wrote to Ernest that "she felt so close to him, it was as if they were one person."[3] Diliberto explains that "He [Hemingway] and Hadley believed their love existed in a realm beyond the physical, where they were spiritual equals" (Diliberto, 79). Pauline Pfeiffer wrote to him: "We are one, we are the same guy, I am you" (Kert, 186). And Martha Gellhorn wrote: " . . . as you are me your work is mine" (Kert, 333). Yet it is above all in Hemingway's imagination—

through his invention of Robert and María—that this language of love finds its truest expression.

Stanton was much closer to the literary reality of the novel when he wrote, "It is the mystic ecstasy evoked by St. John of the Cross [San Juan de la Cruz] but without the old divinity, for María and Jordan have found the gods in each other" (Stanton, 177). Actually it *is* the old divinity, not the old Christian divinity that Stanton means, but a much, much older divinity, the oldest divinity in fact that we know of, the one that inspired, directly or indirectly, Solomon to write the Song of Songs. And in my mind they have not found exactly the "gods" within. I agree with Stanton that "Together, María and the woman of Pablo have opened him [Robert Jordan] to the vast, profound world of the *feminine* which he had resisted in his youth" (Stanton, 187; my emphasis). And I agree when he says, "Through Pilar, and . . . María, *For Whom the Bell Tolls* brought the night mind and a new *feminine* consciousness into Hemingway's work" (Stanton, 172; my emphasis). So the divinity the lovers have found is more properly the ancient ecstatic realm of the Mother-goddess and the Queen of Heaven. What they found, what they plumbed together, timelessly and selflessly and blissfully, was the *goddess* within, especially if we understand this to stand for, as psychologists such as Jung and Erich Neumann have helped us to do, the whole non-rational realm of mystery and intuition.

Andrés and Gómez meet heavy traffic getting to the Estado Mayor where Golz should be, heavy traffic and chaos in the preparations for the offensive. They pass the troops, silent in the dark, and then a staff car flicks on its lights momentarily:

> Andrés saw the troops, steel-helmeted, their rifles vertical, their machine guns pointed up against the dark sky, etched sharp against the night that they dropped into when the light flickered off. Once as he passed close to a troop truck and the lights flashed he saw their faces fixed and sad in the sudden light. (414)

We cannot help being reminded of Goya's great painting of the executions of 3 May 1808, with its sudden yellow light and the faceless

French troops with rifles dark against the sky and the sad face of the peasant hero about to die. Hemingway is here painting his own scenes and disasters of war.

When they reach the top of the pass at Navacerrada, Andrés and Gómez run into André Marty, whom we have already met in our discussion of the real people in the novel. The paranoid Marty, with his gray face that "had a look of decay," his face that "looked as though it were modelled from the waste material you find under the claws of a very old lion" (417), virtually destroys Andrés's mission by needlessly holding him up: "So he sat there with Robert Jordan's dispatch to Golz in his pocket and Gomez and Andrés waited in the guard room and Robert Jordan lay in the woods above the bridge" (423). When Golz finally does get the message all he can say is:

> *Nous sommes foutus. Oui. Comme toujours. Oui. C'est domage. Oui.* It's a shame it came too late. (428)

The untranslated part reads, "We are fucked. Yes. As usual. Yes. It's a shame. Yes." Golz imagines how the attack could have been "if there was no treason and if all did what they should" (429). But such was not the case. As the planes, brought from the Soviet Union and assembled in Spain, come flying over in a deafening roar, he realizes they will bomb ridges with no enemy troops on them, that his brigades are going into an ambush, and that "it would be one famous balls up more." Into the phone, he tells his subordinate Duval, "No. *Rien á faire. Rien. Faut pas penser. Faut accepter.*" (No. Nothing to do. Nothing. No need to think. Just accept [429].) Duval cannot respond: "The roar was such that he could not hear what he was thinking" (430).

13

The Action: Morning of the Fourth Day

The fourth and final morning begins: "Robert Jordan lay behind the trunk of a pine tree on the slope of the hill above the road and the bridge and watched it become daylight." He feels "as though he were a part of the slow lightening that comes before the rising of the sun. . . . " Beneath him "the forest floor was soft and he felt the give of the brown, dropped pine needles under his elbow" (431). Over and again Hemingway emphasizes Jordan's position, prone, on the floor of the forest, part of the earth on which he rests.

Jordan thinks positively in spite of his sense of dread:

> They can't attack any other country until they finish with us and they can never finish with us. . . . Never, if we get anything at all. These people will fight forever if they're well armed. (432)

Jordan sounds positive, but Hemingway, writing after the fact, slips in some irony. They did not "get anything at all" because France, England, and the U.S., the democracies, did absolutely nothing but sit back and watch the fascists take Spain. This is Hemingway's unstated point. These people could not "fight forever" because they were betrayed by their inept leaders, by treason from within, and by lack of support from outside. Jordan thinks, "This is our first big attack" (432), which it was, and it failed; and as soon as it became apparent to the Soviets that they could not engineer a victory, even they pulled out.

Jordan continues positively, "Today is only one day in all the days that will ever be. But what will happen in all the other days that ever come can depend on what you do today" (432). Hemingway continues to have Jordan voice what many would have liked to believe. But Hemingway knows, and within the context of the novel we come to understand, that regardless of Jordan's hedged optimism—notice again that he says "can" depend, not "will" depend—the political treachery of the war undermined and foredoomed the potential in Jordan's phrase. Jordan says "can depend" but Hemingway is saying "could have depended." The ironic tension between what Jordan thinks in May 1937 and what Hemingway knows in 1939–1940 is one of the most subtle and successful devices in the novel. That ironic tension separates Jordan from Hemingway regardless of how many autobiographical traits the author may have given his character.

Hemingway was well aware of their difference and of Jordan's fate. As he wrote to Max Perkins on 13 July 1940, "I hated to have that damned Jordan get what he got after living with the son of a bitch for 17 months" (*Letters*, 506). Then he made a comment in a postscript which inadvertently underscored the difference between Jordan's careful, hedged optimism and his own pessimism, now that "they" were no longer tied up: "There is so much panic and hysteria and shit going around now I don't feel like writing any flagwaving stuff. I will fight but I don't want to write that syndicated patriotism" (*Letters*, 506).

So Jordan lies on the Spanish earth, watching a squirrel and trying not to think. He watches the sentry box and tells himself, "Just do not think at all" (434). Thinking, as we have found out, is not Jordan's favorite activity. First Golz makes fun of thinking: "I never think at all. Why should I? I am *General Sovietique*. I never think" (8). Then Jordan thinks, "Turn off the thinking now, old timer, old comrade. You're a bridge-blower now. Not a thinker" (17). Finally, Golz at the end refines the concept slightly: "*Faut pas penser*" (429), literally, no *need* or *use* to think. And now, once Jordan shoots the sentry, there is simply no time for such reflections.

"You're a bridge-blower now." All that is left is to blow the bridge, and somehow make their escape now that the treacherous Pablo has returned. At this point we might ask, why did Hemingway invent a bridge, why specifically a bridge? Joel Hodson has provided some interesting possibilities. He points out that Hemingway might have had in mind not just Irving Goff, but two other American guerrilla fighters, William Aalto and Alex Kunslick as well. Goff, as we have seen, blew bridges. He and Aalto may have blown a bridge together in 1937 near Teruel, and Kunslick was the only American guerrilla we know was killed behind the lines. Furthermore, if the story of Aalto and Goff is accurate—it was told by Goff twenty-seven years after the fact—it does bear some interesting resemblances to *For Whom the Bell Tolls*: both missions occur "in snow-covered mountains . . . before major Republican offensives"; both took place "at dawn"; both relied on "an old peasant guide"; and both ended "in a running firefight . . . pursued by enemy cavalry."[1]

Hodson is not convinced by the similarities, however, and argues instead a plausible case for T. E. Lawrence's having influenced the novel. Hemingway knew Lawrence's writing well. Of that there is no doubt since he included "Blowing Up a Train" as one of two excerpts from Lawrence's *Seven Pillars of Wisdom* in his war anthology, *Men At War*. Hodson goes on to point out a number of interesting similarities between Jordan and Lawrence: both blow up trains; both are outsiders working behind the lines; both must convince native partisans of their missions in the face of treachery; both learn that the enemy is aware of the larger operation; both have written books about their respective cultures; both are "amateur soldiers" who have become "demolition experts"; and both have to blow bridges (Hodson, 7–9).

There are obvious differences, too. The fictional Jordan is about to die; the real Lawrence is not. Jordan blows his bridge; Lawrence does not. There are other differences, too, which Hodson does not point out, such as the differences in attitude between Lawrence and Jordan. Lawrence sometimes treats his Arabs as ignorant inferiors; Jordan does not. And Jordan learns a great deal from his partisans, including nothing less than the meaning of love. In the end, Hodson does not so much prove that Jordan was modeled on Lawrence—and in my mind, he was not—as that, as men of action in similar situations, they have some very similar duties and circumstances.

At one point Hodson remarks that Hemingway "was not a combatant nor did he have much personal knowledge of guerrilla warfare at that time" (Hodson, 3). What then are we to make of the splendid Robert Capa photograph of Hemingway in the front lines during the battle of Teruel helping a Republican soldier get his rifle unjammed? Hemingway described the episode in one of his dispatches: " . . . we broke for the ridge where the advanced positions of the center were. In a little while it was not a nice place either, although the view was splendid and the soldier I was lying next to was having trouble with his rifle. It jammed after every shot and I showed him how to knock the bolt open with a rock" (Watson 1988, 65; see frontispiece). And in a letter to his great military friend General Buck Lanham, Hemingway "strongly implied he had actually fought with the Loyalists in 1937" (Baker 1969, 512). Also José Luis Herrera Sotolongo, Hemingway's physician in Cuba and a surgeon for the Loyalists, claimed Hemingway "liked to get in the trenches and fight. He did so in Guadalajara and Jarama" (Fuentes, 155).

Hemingway certainly had personal knowledge of combat, even if he was not exactly a combatant, but what about guerrilla warfare? William Braasch Watson has published a series of articles devoted to precisely that question. His answer is not surprising: Hemingway knew a great deal more about guerrilla warfare than anyone had so far given him credit. He may have even gone on a behind-the-lines mission himself.

Watson became interested because of an account by a Pole named Anton Chrost that appeared in 1989 in Aleksander Szurek's *The Shattered Dream*, an account that claimed that Chrost was the model for Jordan. Here is Watson's version of the story:

> Chrost's story, as told to Szurek, goes like this: One day Ernest Hemingway showed up at Chrost's guerrilla headquarters in the little town of Alfambra just to the north of Teruel and made a nui-

sance of himself questioning Chrost about his guerrilla operations behind the Fascist lines. Several weeks later, Hemingway showed up again, this time for four days, with authorization to take part in a guerrilla operation. After a few days of preparation, Hemingway accompanied Chrost and his partisans as they crossed the mountains into enemy territory northwest of Teruel and blew up a train that was heading toward the Rebel-held city. Hemingway and the partisans all got back safely to their own lines, had a big meal at their headquarters, and the next day, just before leaving to go back to wherever he had come from, Hemingway told Chrost he was going to write about him in his book. But he was going to make Chrost, the Pole, into an American, he said.[2]

Watson, a trained historian, was naturally skeptical to begin with:

To say that I was surprised by Chrost's story is putting it perhaps too mildly and simply, for I was at once both fascinated by the vivid details with which it was told and astounded that at this late date somebody could come forward with a story like this and expect anybody to believe it. I was intrigued that here for the first time was an eyewitness account of Hemingway's direct involvement with guerrilla warfare in Spain—something everyone has always assumed he never had—and yet I was put on guard by the incongruous nature of the story, coming as it did from such an unexpected source and being told so artfully that it seemed more like a tale out of the Grimm brothers than an actual event. (Watson, Winter 1991, 39)

What is surprising is how much of the story Watson has been able to substantiate and, conversely, how little he could repudiate. He does not believe that Chrost was an exact model for Jordan but that Jordan is made of "bits and pieces . . . including not a little from his own [Hemingway's] past" (Watson, Winter 1991, 40). But Watson has been able to prove that Hemingway knew a great deal about guerrilla warfare, and he makes a very strong circumstantial argument for Hemingway's having participated clandestinely in Chrost's mission.

Watson has found out: that Hemingway did, in fact, visit Alfambra on 20 September 1937; that Chrost's details of the mission were accurate; that Hemingway obtained shortly thereafter an unusual safe-conduct good for *todos los sectores* (all sectors) from 27 October through 27 November 1937 (Watson reproduces the pass); that Hemingway did in fact take a trip from 27 or 28 October until 2 November 1937, putatively to Alicante to get mail, for which he had a chauffeur and access to two cars; that the mileage to both Alicante and Alfambra, via Valencia, was almost the same; and that there was no evidence at all that he went to Alicante or flew from Alicante to Paris for mail, which was the usual procedure (Watson, Winter 1991, 44–66).

In his second article, Watson went a good deal further. He actually reconstructed Hemingway's trip, in the process determining: that Hemingway took the Dodge (the Opel's gas tank was too small); that the Dodge could have made the trip easily with extra petrol cans; that Szurek's version of Chrost's story was viable; that the mission involved blowing a railway bridge over the Jiloca River; that their objective was actually the train crossing the bridge more than the bridge itself; that they hiked the twenty-five kilometers each way to the bridge and back, crossing the lines in the process; that Hemingway learned a great deal about the techniques for blowing a bridge; that they blew the bridge without incident—"The train blew up as it went over the bridge, completely shattering some cars, and everyone took off for the Republican lines, with Hemingway keeping close to the others"; and that they "arrived at their headquarters before daylight," and celebrated with "a big meal of roast lamb and wine."[3] Hemingway told Chrost that in the book he would be an American, and then said something that rings very true: he told Chrost he "did not know for certain what kind of book he would be writing on the war in Spain" (Watson, Summer 1991, 92).

In his third article, Watson examines *For Whom the Bell Tolls* in light of what he has learned. He believes Hemingway had "secretly returned to Alfambra . . . as a writer in search of material for a book, and as a writer he had kept the trip to Alfambra a secret for the rest of his life."[4] When Hemingway told his friend Ben Finney he had made it all up, it was true enough; but as usual he had invented it from some amalgam of experience. To the extent that Watson is correct about Hemingway's activities, we can say that some of the startlingly clear sense of reality the novel has, comes from those experiences. And as Watson explains, Hemingway had no books on guerrilla activity in the Spanish Civil War—the way he had for the retreat from Caporetto in *A Farewell to Arms*—because none had been published yet.

Watson decided to focus on the central event of the novel, the blowing of the bridge, which as he comments is "anticipated by the reader and prepared for by Hemingway from the first pages of the novel" (Watson 1992, 5). He then proceeded to consult a series of experts on demolition and to report the following on their conclusions: that Hemingway had given Jordan the proper background; that Jordan's use of sketches was proper technique; that his separation of materials was scientifically sound and essential for safety; that Jordan, properly, carried a bit more explosives than he needed; that his equipment was accurately described and in order, down to fine details; that grenades in lieu of the exploder and detonating caps stolen by Pablo were dangerous but effective; that the description of the bridge going down was "very accurate and believable"; that, over all, "Hemingway had acquired a detailed and thorough knowledge of the subtleties of demolition work and that he had accurately communicated this knowledge throughout his novel in ways that were both subtle and realistic" (Watson 1992, 6–26).

Watson also located the field manual that Hemingway probably used for such details as Jordan's cigar box, his use of separate backpacks, or the reason why he carried more explosives than necessary. Hemingway had the book, titled *Engineer Field Manual* (published in New York by the Military Publishing Company) in his library in Cuba. But the manual did not provide all of Hemingway's information. Watson concludes finally that Hemingway must have been with Chrost in order to know as much as he did both about the culture and the technique of the guerrilla fighters: "There could not be much doubt that Hemingway had drawn heavily on somebody's knowledge and experience of demolition work, and that somebody was almost certainly Antek Chrost" (Watson 1992, 39). Watson's articles are sure to be controversial because they are circumstantial; but they are powerfully circumstantial, and they prove beyond doubt that, wherever he got the information from, Hemingway knew exactly what he was writing about.

Robert E. Gajdusek, whose mythic interpretation of Pilar's tale I have already noted, provides a possibly interesting piece of unintentional corroboration to Watson's thesis. Gajdusek sees bridges as "the supreme metaphoric expression . . . [of] the principal of total ambiguity" in all of Hemingway's work.[5] Specifically he sees an ironic bridge-building in the destruction of the bridge:

> We are carefully permitted to see that to wire the bridge for destruction is to connect both sides and to interweave between sunlight and shadow, uniting the above world of the sky with the dark world of the ravine. Indeed, as the bridge goes, that which was cut off above is united with that below; Pilar (above) and Pablo (below) join one another and, at the end, bracing María between them, they disappear over the hill. (Gajdusek 1983, 78)

Admittedly this is a symbolic interpretation, but it is interesting to note that the only technique Watson's experts objected to at all was the wiring technique Jordan used, with a wire for each side of the bridge, precisely the basis for Gajdusek's symbolic vision (left side-right side; rational-intuitive) of bridging while demolishing. At one point Pilar screams impatiently "Is he building a bridge or blowing one?" (444). Gajdusek observes, "of course the former is the case" (Gajdusek 1983, 78), a symbolic judgment that fits perfectly with the novel's epigraph "No man is an *Island*" (i.e., he is bridged to *Mankinde*). If both Watson and Gajdusek are right, the only time Hemingway pushed the credibility of the technique of demolition even the least bit was in order to render a deeper meaning to his story, turning the destruction of the physical bridge into the construction of a spiritual bridge.

Hemingway himself never clarified any of this, except to relate to Max Perkins his enthusiasm and confidence:

The last chapter is the most exciting in the book. It's almost
unbearably exciting during and after the bridge is blown. I finished the part where—what the hell—will not tell you—you can
read it—I was as limp and dead as though it had all happened to
me. Anyhow it is a hell of a book. I knew I had to write a hell of a
last chapter. (*Letters*, 506)

Observe now as Jordan blows his bridge to see if there are two
sides or if there is an above and a below and light and dark (my emphasis throughout). Jordan begins, "thinking only of demolition, working
fast and skillfully as a surgeon works," lashing one *side*, then climbing
"*through* the trestling, like a bloody Tarzan in a rolled steel forest . . .
and then coming *out from under the dark*, the stream tumbling *below*
him," feeling the air *beneath* the bridge "cool as a wine *cellar*" and
clean: "This is a *dream* bridge. A bloody *dream* bridge" (436–37).
Talking to himself he lashes the *other side*: "You're shaking like a
Goddamn woman. What the hell is the matter with you? You're trying
to do it too fast. I'll bet that Goddamn woman up *above* isn't shaking.
That *Pilar*" (437). Then he leans "*out and up into the sunlight* . . . his
head now *above* the noise of the *falling water*" (437). As he goes back
under he thinks of Pablo, "That son of a bitch threw my exploder *in the
river. . . . In this river* he threw it. That bastard Pablo. He gave them hell
below just now" (437). Then Jordan links his present with his past,
becoming conscious through an allusion to a gospel hymn of the symbolism of his name: "You and your head. You have a nice thinking head
old Jordan. Roll Jordan, Roll! They used to yell that at football when
you lugged the ball. Do you know the damned Jordan is really not
much bigger than that creek down there *below* . . . " (438).

Let's add it up: *thinking* and working like a surgeon on a *dream*
bridge; the sun above, the river below, Pilar above, Pablo below, the
two sides of the bridge, past and present, with memories of the young
Jordan rolling toward the End Zone, and the River Jordan, which
Joshua crossed over to lead the Children of Israel to the Promised
Land and in whose waters John baptized Jesus, enacting through the
old Hebrew ritual of purification the sacrament that for Christians rep-
resented the bridge to the Promised Land of Heaven, or as the gospel

hymn "Roll, Jordan, Roll" puts it: "I want to go to Heaven when I die/to hear Jordan roll."[6] And doesn't Jordan think of this connection just at the moment when he is destroying the old bridge, washing away the old into the waters of the river below, in order to build the new spiritual one, some 447 pages into the novel?

H. R. Stoneback has pointed out that in the phrase (or title) "Roll Jordan, Roll!" Hemingway "utters explicitly the significance of the protagonist's patronymic which functions implicitly as a sign from the moment the reader first learns his name" (Stoneback, 105). A second reading of the novel with the knowledge that the last name Jordan is such a sign substantiates that we are meant to have suspected what the name Jordan alluded to all along. If not Hemingway would not have confirmed it in the book's climactic moments just before Jordan blows the bridge.

While Jordan is finishing the final preparations, Anselmo is waiting and thinking about the sentry he has just killed: "That is over, he told himself, and thou canst try to atone for it as for the others" (443). He thinks, "If I die on this morning it is all right," and as he waits, Hemingway describes him as "not lonely nor . . . in any way alone":

> He was *one* with the wire in his hand and *one* with the bridge, and *one* with the charges the *Inglés* had placed. He was *one* with the *Inglés* still working under the bridge and he was *one* with all of the battle and with the Republic. (433; my emphasis)

Anselmo wants to *atone* and he is *at-oned*, that is, he is integrated, *one* with everything around him. Such integration is mortal and he will reach his atonement by dying, perishing with the bridge. As Stoneback reminds us, Anselmo

> . . . has certain traits in common with Saint Anselm, including age and dignity and the reputation of a wise and reformist (not radical) commitment to his cause. Most striking, perhaps, is the fact that Saint Anselm's most famous work, *Cur Deus Homo*, was the most important medieval contribution to the theology of atonement, and the expiation motif in the novel centers on Anselmo. (Stoneback, 104)

Jordan yells to Anselmo, "Blow her!" and together they pull the wires on either side to destroy the bridge: " . . . and then there was a cracking roar and the middle of the bridge rose up in the air like a wave breaking . . . " (445).

When Jordan finds Anselmo dead, he is full of anger, emptiness, and hate. Gradually, however, his rage fades:

> Once you saw it again as it was to others, once you get rid of your own *self*, the always ridding of *self* that you had to do in war. Where there could be no *self*. Where *yourself* is only to be lost. (447; my emphasis)

Jordan's ridding of self, the cathartic purgation of self and selfishness, is an important step in *his* impending integration.

María, guarding the horses, prays for Jordan before the blowing of the bridge:

> Then she commenced to pray for Roberto quickly and automatically as she had done at school, saying the prayers as fast as she could and counting them on the fingers of her left hand, praying by tens of each of the two prayers she was repeating. (449)

After the bridge blows she prays directly:

> Oh please have him be all right for all my heart and all of me is at the bridge. . . . Oh, Sweet Blessed Virgin, bring him back to me from the bridge and I will do anything thou sayest ever. Because I am not here. There isn't any me. I am only with him. Take care of him for me and that will be me . . . (449–50).

"There isn't any me": María too is ridding herself of self. Jordan is cleansing himself of self-indulgence and hatred. If he does not, he cannot give himself for María. If she is not prepared—selfless as well—she cannot accept his gift. When they were in la gloria, Hemingway had written and then deleted, perhaps because it told too much, a phrase I have already noted but that comes inevitably to mind here: "only by giving can it be received" (KL:EH 83, 36–5).

The Action: Morning of the Fourth Day

As the Luftwaffe planes from Segovia begin to bomb the incipient offensive, Jordan has a kind of precognitive vision:

> He had the feeling of something that had started normally and had then brought great, outsized, giant repercussions. It was as though you had thrown a stone and the stone made a ripple and the ripple returned roaring and toppling as a tidal wave. Or as though you shouted and the echo came back in rolls and peals of thunder, and the thunder was deadly. Or as though you struck one man and he fell and as far as you could see other men rose up all armed and armored. He was glad he was not with Golz up at the pass. (451)

If we disregard the last sentence, we can suspect that Hemingway had much more in mind here than the offensive on Segovia and the Nationalist response. Jordan's stone has concentricities that spread outward from Spain to World War II and to all the armed conflicts still going on today.

When Pablo arrives, those that remain of the band—Pilar, Pablo, Jordan, María, Agustín, Rafael and Primitivo, all the rest dead—prepare to ride to the Gredos Mountains in the west. But first they must cross the road.

Jordan crosses last, and as he and his big gray horse—the big gray from whose back he had shot the Navarrese cavalryman the morning before—head up the far bank, almost to safety, Jordan looks back down at the bridge and sees "the bright flash from the heavy, squat, mud-colored tank there on the road." And then he goes down with the horse on top of him, "and he was under the gray horse and the gray horse was kicking and he was trying to pull out from under the weight" (460–61).

His left leg is broken from where the horse had rolled on him, "as though there was a new joint in it; not the hip joint but another one that went sideways like a hinge." The horse knees himself up, and Jordan, his right leg slipping clear, can feel "the sharp bone and where it pressed against the skin" (461). Primitivo and Agustín grab him under the arms and drag him up out of the tank's range, but his left thigh bone has snapped ten inches below the hip, and "he could feel the snapped-off thigh bone tight against the skin" (462).

Now Robert Jordan must say goodbye to María and convince her to go with Pablo and Pilar. What he tells her echoes everything they have learned together:

> . . . I go always with thee wherever thou goest. . . . As long as there is one of us there is both of us. . . . Whichever one there is, is both. . . . But I am thee also now. . . . Now you will go for us both. . . . You are me now. . . . we both go in thee. . . . Thou art all there will be of me. (463–64)

In commenting on John Donne's sense of love and death, Warren Shibles wrote a brief description that applies just as well to what Hemingway is expressing in this passage: "If there was balance one could conquer death, if not, not. If lovers part, it is like a death but if in harmony, there can be no death. Love can, in a way, conquer physical death."[7] If, in the glorious figures of love, one and one is one, now two minus one is still two. Jordan tells her that what he does he must do alone: "That people cannot do together. Each one must do it alone" (463), and he sends her off between Pilar and Pablo with the words: "I am with thee now. We are both there. Go!" (465).

Then Jordan must prepare himself to kill and to die, to use up what is left of him for her, to give what is left of him for her, to sacrifice himself for her: *"And if you wait and hold them up even a little while or just get the officer that may make all the difference. One thing well done can make—"* (470).

Jordan lies there waiting, in pain now from having turned over onto his elbow and stomach; at times "slipping away from himself as you feel snow starting to slip sometimes on a mountain slope" (471); fighting off the temptation to kill himself; talking to the ancestral figure of his grandfather to bolster his strength; wondering if orthodox belief would help; not fearing death now; believing the things he had told María: "It *is* sort of the way I said. It is really very much that way" (469). As all these things go through his mind, Jordan feels *integrated*:

> He was completely integrated now and he took a good long look
> at everything. Then he looked up at the sky. There were big white
> clouds in it. He touched the palm of his hand against the pine
> needles where he lay and he touched the bark of the pine trunk he
> lay behind. (471)

"Integrated": I do not know of another use of that word, certainly not in this sense, in Hemingway's work. *Integrated*: knowing la gloria; having felt the earth move; being selfless and giving completely of
himself; accepting that he can have had his whole life in seventy hours;
believing now in the intuitive along with the rational, the female side of
him and the male, the dark along with the light; feeling himself a part
of humanity, bridged to John Donne's *Mankinde*; lying on the Spanish
earth in touch with nature; sacrificing; saving. The wheel has come
around now, all the way, but in its last orbit Jordan has learned a great
deal: "Christ, I was learning fast there at the end" (467).

Integrated now, he can die. And he knows it. He had said as
much to himself just before positioning himself for the bridge:

> He knew he himself was nothing, and he knew death was noth-
> ing. He knew that truly, as truly as he knew anything. In the last
> few days he had learned that he himself, with another person,
> could be everything. But inside himself he knew that this was the
> exception. That we have had, he thought. In that I have been
> most fortunate. That was given to me, perhaps, because I never
> asked for it. That cannot be taken nor lost. (393)

Jordan knows it and he understands how rare it is. His integration—a phenomenon spelled out far more clearly than is usually the
case with Hemingway—was something that Hemingway himself probably experienced most fully here and now in the great undiscovered
country of his own imagination, an experience which may explain why
he felt it was so exciting. Jordan has a vision, a vision of Madrid "Just
over the hills there, and down across the plain. Down out of the gray
rocks and the pines, the heather and the gorse, across the yellow high
plateau you see it rising white and beautiful" (467). That vision is
more like a new Jerusalem than like the real Madrid (which is not and

was not white at all). And he suddenly has come at least to respect and recognize Pilar's visions: "She was afraid maybe I believed it. I don't though. But she does. They see something. Or they feel something. Like a bird dog" (467).

Integrated, envisioning, and understanding, Robert Jordan—the most complete character Hemingway created—is "holding onto himself very carefully and delicately," as he lies waiting for Lt. Berrendo to reach "the sunlit place where the first trees of the pine forest joined the green slope of the meadow." *For Whom the Bell Tolls* ends as Robert Jordan feels "his heart beating against the pine needle floor of the forest" (471). The wheel has come full circle from forest floor to forest floor, but this time Jordan feels "his heart beating."

In leaving Jordan there, calmly awaiting his own death, but suspended in time, frozen in prose, at the exact point where the Spanish earth wheels back to the Spanish earth, Hemingway accomplishes two significant things. Jordan's heart, absent from the beginning description, becomes our final image; and it is the hero's heart, the beating of which still gives him life. It is the lover's heart, which he has found in this round of seventy hours. And Jordan does not die, he does not quite ever discover that undiscovered country from whose bourn no traveler returns. In *Death in the Afternoon*, Hemingway wrote that "all stories, if continued far enough, end in death" (*DIA*, 122). This story does not continue quite that far, and the undiscovered country of death remains intentionally undisclosed.

When I brought up this idea at our Moscow meeting, Michael Reynolds remarked, "Art stops time—it's the only thing that does." By giving up his idea for an epilogue to tie up the loose ends, Hemingway was able to leave Robert Jordan there on the Spanish earth, at the still point of the turning world, in that eternal present, his heart still beating, suspended artfully on the edge of death just as the lovers were suspended in ecstasy, undefeated by time. Only in the true undiscovered country of the imagination—Hemingway's and through his, ours—can such a vicarious release from human bondage and mortality take place. But that is of course precisely why the artist writes and why we read. And our remembrance of *For Whom the Bell Tolls* bears an unmistakable resemblance to the memory of Robert Jordan that María carries away with her, always.

Appendix: On Language

In the long section that Hemingway cut from the last chapter of *Death in the Afternoon*, he remarked on the difficulties involved in writing about Spain:

> In the first place I am not Spanish and I did not know the language. It took a while to learn even to speak it. You had to get rid of Italian, all of it. After I could talk, read, and understand it I still knew I did not know it.[1]

Seven years later, when he wrote *For Whom the Bell Tolls*, Hemingway still did not "know" Spanish, just as he would not after living for many years in Cuba, as his letters and the few extant recordings of him bear out. His letters show mistakes of all kinds, and his speech was, while somewhat fluent, full of errors and heavily Anglo-Saxon-sounding. As late as 6 June 1959, Hemingway joked in a letter to his good friend Juanito Quintana (Montoya in *The Sun Also Rises*) that he could not write in Spanish because he suffered from "analfabetismo agudo con derrame," "acute illiteracy with hemorrhaging" (KL:EH, outgoing correspondence).

In 1976 I wrote a paper on Hemingway's poor Spanish (alluded to in text, published in 1983), pointing out that there were more than sixty different errors (not repetitions, distinct errors) in the Spanish in *For Whom the Bell Tolls*. My conclusions were somewhat exaggerated, but the errors have not gone away, and we need to deal with them, even if briefly.

There are two kinds of Spanish in the novel: the Spanish rendered in English and the Spanish actually in Spanish. All the dialogue in the novel (as opposed to the narration or Jordan's thoughts) takes place in Spanish unless otherwise indicated, such as the following:

> In English he whispered very quietly, "I'd like to marry you, rabbit. I'm very proud of your family." (355)

The "Spanish" in English has struck readers in different ways. Martha Gellhorn, who was the first to hear any of it, told Spanish novelist Juan Benet and me, nearly fifty years after the fact, "I was with him, of course, when he was writing it and he read me the first part when he'd finished. I thought that literally translated Spanish was awful and I told him so. Well that was the last he read me. Because, you see, I had dared to be critical."[2] Nor did Colin Wilson like his "device of conversation that is supposed to be literally translated" very much: "As far as I am concerned, Hemingway has never sounded so inauthentic as in this type of dialogue: 'I obscenity in the milk of thy obscenity' etc."[3]

John J. Allen, a professor of Spanish, wrote in 1961 that "while the English of Hemingway's Spaniards is anything but an objectively accurate rendition of the original, it reflects dynamically the author's impressions both of the people and of their language."[4] On the other hand, Joseph Warren Beach believed that Hemingway had accomplished "a linguistic feat of the first magnitude," and that he had "added another 'dimension' to his English prose."[5]

Clearly just how well this highly original style works depends on the individual reader or critic's ear and knowledge, or lack thereof, of Spanish. Betty Moore, after working through and categorizing many of the devices used in the style, including Hemingway's inconsistencies and errors, thinks that Hemingway was working more for effect than for realism and that "However incorrect Hemingway's Spanish, it was sufficient for his purpose, which was simply to carry over the speech patterns and rhythm into English."[6]

Probably we could leave it at that, except for one "error" that has been a critical bone of contention since Arturo Barea first pointed it out in the May issue of *Horizon* in 1941. Robert Jordan's nickname for María is "rabbit," and "rabbit," to quote Barea, is "one of the more frequent and vulgar euphemisms for the female sexual organ," the use of which in public "would have provoked a truly Rabelaisian outburst" (Barea, 88).

Once we know this—and there is simply no doubt about what it means—we are left with two possibilities: 1) that Hemingway knew what it meant and used it anyway or even intentionally; and 2) that Hemingway was ignorant of this particular euphemism and therefore unintentionally put Robert Jordan, the Spanish professor, in a somewhat awkward position. I no longer believe the second possibility ruins the novel because in taking it as a work of the imagination, I can understand that Hemingway's invention from experience was insufficient linguistically but not imaginatively. Certainly it is an unfortunate coincidence, but I think I know where it originates. Considered in its proper context, its meaning can be interpreted positively.

If we assume that Hemingway did not know what it meant, all we have to do is understand the poetic value of the innocent nickname. Rabbit has an interesting history in Hemingway's fiction.

In "Cross Country Snow" Nick Adams runs into soft snow and spills, going "over and over in a clashing of skis, feeling like a shot rabbit . . . " (*CSS*, 143). In the original ending to "Big Two-Hearted River," published posthumously as "On Writing," Nick finds a stunned rabbit in the woods, removes a tick from the rabbit, and releases it. As he does so, "He felt its heart beating as he laid it down" (*NAS*, 241). Nick and the rabbit, two creatures in the woods, each with a heart: perhaps that is one reason Hemingway changed the name of the real river, the Fox, to the fictional "Big Two-Hearted River" (there is a Two Hearted River nearby, but no "Big" version of it).

In *Green Hills of Africa* there is a wonderful scene in which some Masai warriors run down a rabbit and then present it to Hemingway as a tribute: "I held him and could feel the thumping of his heart through the soft, warm, furry body. . . . " Hemingway hands the rabbit to his tracker who gives it to one of the Masai who lets it go: "The Masai stooped and put the rabbit on the ground and as he ran free they all laughed" (*GHA*, 220).

As mentioned in chapter nine, in two unpublished fragments a Hemingway-like character calls a Martha Gellhorn-like character "rabbit." Within the novel there are many allusions to rabbits and hares. Anselmo tells of being shot at early in the war "as though we were rabbits" (42). When El Sordo is trapped on the hill waiting for the planes to come, he feels naked: "There is no nakeder thing than I feel, he thought. A flayed rabbit is as well covered as a bear in comparison" (310).

When Robert and María meet, she serves him "rabbit cooked with onions and green peppers and there were chick peas in the red wine sauce. It was well cooked, the rabbit meat flaked off the bones, and the sauce was delicious" (22–23). This is a common enough dish in the region. The last time I ate in Segovia, at the historic Mesón de Cándido, the *plato del día* was a delicious rabbit cooked in red wine. Yet Hemingway uses this rabbit business for more than local color. The next time they eat hares that were tracked through the snow and that were mating when the Gypsy killed them.

Rabbits are obviously a fragile part of the natural world. Rabbits, hares, other animals, the grain fields, the mountains, all are meant to be parts of a natural, innocent and pure world of which María, whose name connotes innocence and purity, is a part. "Rabbit" in English suggests that very well. In *Green Hills of Africa*, Hemingway remarked that "A continent ages quickly once we come. The natives live in harmony with it" (284). The guerrillas are something like "the natives," living still in a world in harmony with nature. María belongs to that vanishing world that is being destroyed by the mechanized doom of the war with no more regard for human life than for a rabbit's.

On the other hand, what if Hemingway did know what it meant? Gajdusek has the only possible positive answer: "That María is also "Rabbit" tells us she is a priestess of spirit *and* flesh, of heavenly transcendence *and* biological reproductive cycle, that she at one and the same moment abandons *and* establishes the terms of nature" (Gajdusek 1983, 80; my emphasis).

This issue of Hemingway's knowledge or ignorance is probably unresolvable—although I prefer to think he was ignorant—but it brings up a larger issue. Carlos Baker reports that Republican General Gustavo Durán, in exile in the U.S. after the end of the Spanish Civil War, read the galleys "to make sure that the Spanish was correct . . . and was not much impressed by the quality of Ernesto's Spanish" (Baker 1969, 350–51). Robert Van Gelder in an interview published in the *New York Times* (11 August 1940), when Hemingway was finishing reading proof, reports that Hemingway said, "Now that I've finally found him [Durán], the book is on its way to the printer, can't be changed." Only days later (26 August), Hemingway would write to Max Perkins regarding Spanish names, "Follow my corrected galleys on this without querying them. I have checked all usage carefully" (*Letters*, 516). Finally, he would tell Charles Scribner in October, after the book came out, "I am catching a bunch of errors in the book for when your plates wear out" (*Letters*, 520).

Durán obviously did not read, or at least did not correct, the galleys. Hemingway did not check the usage carefully. And the plates have not worn out. Now part of this is undoubtedly Hemingway's own fault. But over a period of years as the late Jim Hinkle of San Diego State and I discussed this issue, Hinkle convinced me that a good deal of the blame rested with people at Scribner's who should have "protected him," as Hinkle put it in a letter to me, "from his gaps in knowledge" (2 July 1982).

Scott Berg titled his biography of Max Perkins *Editor of Genius*, and Perkins no doubt did edit the work of geniuses—Fitzgerald, Thomas Wolfe, Hemingway. As editor, however, he does not appear to have been such a genius, and Charles Scribner, as publisher, does not appear much better. James R. Mellow, in his biography of F. Scott Fitzgerald points out that Perkins's "slackness about editorial standards" only made Fitzgerald look like a worse writer than he was. Mellow cites the critic Henry Seidel Canby, who asked, "Is it laziness, indifference, a lack of standards, or imperfect education that results in this constant botching of the first-rate by American novelists?" And he cites Clifton Fadiman, who listed in the *New Yorker* "the misspellings in French and English, in the names of psychiatrists, physicians, and medical diagnoses (*schizzoid* for *schizoid*, for instance), composers, place names and types of liqueurs, and made the most pertinent case against the sloppy proofreading and editorial supervision" of *Tender Is the Night*.[7] Add to all of the above errors in Spanish and French in virtually all of Hemingway's work and the sixty-odd errors in Spanish in *For Whom the Bell Tolls* alone, and the case against Perkins and company is strong. Our best novelists deserved then, and now, better treatment.

In the final analysis, readers will have to judge for themselves in these matters and determine individually just how the errors, and the blame for them, affect one's own reading. Stanton observes that, "Failing to see the forest for a single tree, some critics have gone to the extreme of claiming that María's nickname ruins the entire novel" (Stanton, 159). He means me, and he is correct to object. As Hemingway wrote in that letter to Faulkner about *For Whom the Bell Tolls*, "Anyway is as good as I can write and was takeing all chances (for a pitcher who, when has control, can throw fairly close) could take. (Probably failed)" (*Letters*, 624). He did not fail, of course, and that is the point. Even if he did throw an occasional wild pitch in Spanish now and then, he won the game. And he had the last word. As he put it in that letter to Faulkner in his most eloquent prose, "Found good country outside, learned language as well as know English, and lost it the same way" (*Letters*, 624).

Notes and References

Introduction

1. Carlos Baker, *Ernest Hemingway: A Life Story* (New York: Charles Scribner's Sons, 1969), 348; hereafter cited in text as Baker 1969.

1. Historical Context: The Writer's Problem

1. *Ernest Hemingway, Selected Letters, 1917–1961*, ed. Carlos Baker (New York: Charles Scribner's Sons, 1981), 456–58. Hereafter cited in text as *Letters*.

2. Carlos Baker, *The Writer as Artist*, 4th ed. (Princeton, N.J.: Princeton University Press, 1972), 241; hereafter cited in text as Baker 1972.

3. Ernest Hemingway, *For Whom the Bell Tolls* (New York: Charles Scribner's Sons, 1940), 43; all page references in text are to this edition.

2. Importance of the Work: No Man Is an Island

1. Allen Josephs, "*Toreo*: The Moral Axis of *The Sun Also Rises*," *The Hemingway Review* 6.1 (Fall 1986): 99.

3. Critical Reception: Here Is a Mountain

1. Michael S. Reynolds, *Hemingway's Reading, 1910–1940: An Inventory* (Princeton, N.J.: Princeton University Press, 1981), 83. I am grateful to Professor William Braasch Watson for pointing this out to me at the Moscow Conference.

2. Alvah C. Bessie, "A postscript," in *The Merrill Studies in* For Whom the Bell Tolls, ed. Sheldon Norman Grebstein (Columbus, Ohio: Merrill, 1971), 13; hereafter cited in text.

4. Spain: The Undiscovered Country

1. Malcolm Cowley, "A Portrait of Mr. Papa," *Life* (10 January 1949); hereafter cited in text.

2. Gregory Hemingway, *Papa: A Personal Memoir* (Boston: Houghton Mifflin, 1976), 23.

3. Ernest Hemingway, *Death in the Afternoon* (New York: Charles Scribner's Sons, 1932), 2–3; hereafter cited in text as *DIA*.

5. Politics: Discovery and Abandonment

1. *By-Line: Ernest Hemingway*, ed. William White (New York: Charles Scribner's Sons, 1967), 64; hereafter cited in text.

2. Ernest Hemingway, "The Art of the Short Story," *Paris Review* 23, no. 79 (Spring 1981): 93.

3. Bernice Kert, *The Hemingway Women* (New York: W. W. Norton & Co., 1983), 299; hereafter cited in text.

6. The Real War: Treachery and Rotten-ness

1. Ernest Hemingway, *The Complete Short Stories of Ernest Hemingway* (New York: Charles Scribner's Sons, 1987), 420; hereafter cited in text as *CSS*.

2. Martin Light, "Of Wasteful Deaths: Hemingway's Stories About the Spanish War," in *The Short Stories of Ernest Hemingway: Critical Essays*, ed. Jackson J. Benson (Durham, N.C.: Duke University Press, 1975), 77.

7. The Invented War: Telling a Story

1. Gabriel García Márquez, "The Visual Arts, the Poetization of Space and Writing: An Interview with Gabriel García Márquez." Interview by Raymond Leslie Williams, *PMLA* 104.2: 131–40; hereafter cited in text.

2. Arturo Barea, "Not Spain but Hemingway," in *The Merrill Studies in* For Whom the Bell Tolls, ed. Sheldon Norman Grebstein (Columbus, Ohio: Merrill, 1971), 80-90. First published in the May 1941 issue of *Horizon*.

3. Julio Alvarez del Vayo, *Give Me Combat* (Boston: Little Brown, 1973), 188.

4. Juan Benet, in conversation, Michigan State University Conference: International Literature of the Spanish Civil War, 21 November 1987.

5. Allen Josephs, "Hemingway's Poor Spanish: Chauvinism and Loss of Credibility in *For Whom the Bell Tolls*," in *Hemingway: A Revaluation*, ed. Donald R. Noble (Troy, N.Y.: Whitston, 1983): 205–23.

6. Martha Gellhorn, in conversation, Michigan State University

Conference: International Literature of the Spanish Civil War, 21 November 1987. See Appendix for further comments by Martha Gellhorn.

7. Robert A. Martin, "Hemingway's *For Whom the Bell Tolls*: Fact into Fiction," *Studies in American Fiction* 15.2: 219–25; hereafter cited in text.

8. Michael J. B. Allen, "The Unspanish War in *For Whom the Bell Tolls*, *Contemporary Literature* 13.2 (Spring 1972): 204–12.

9. The Ernest Hemingway Collection, Item no. 83. The collection is in the John F. Kennedy Library at Columbia Point, Boston; hereafter cited in text as KL/EH.

8. The Setting: The Country You Know

1. William Braasch Watson, "Hemingway's Spanish Civil War Dispatches, "*The Hemingway Review* 7.2 (Spring 1988): 36–37; hereafter cited in text as Watson 1988.

2. A. E. Hotchner, *Papa Hemingway* (New York: Random House, 1966), 131; hereafter cited in text.

3. Mary Welsh Hemingway, *How It Was* (New York: Alfred A. Knopf, 1976), 333.

4. Hugh Thomas, *The Spanish Civil War* (New York: Harper and Row, 1977), 689; hereafter cited in text.

5. Angel Capellán, *Hemingway and the Hispanic World* (Ann Arbor, Mich.: UMI Research Press, 1985), 25; hereafter cited in text.

6. José Luis Castillo-Puche, *Hemingway in Spain*, trans. Helen R. Lane (Garden City, N.Y.: Doubleday, 1974), 309.

7. Peter Wyden, *The Passionate War: The Narrative History of the Spanish Civil War, 1936–1939* (New York: Simon and Schuster, 1983), 277; Wyden's ellipses; hereafter cited in text.

8. Letter from William Braasch Watson, 3 April 1993.

9. The Characters: Instead of Just a Hero

1. Jeffrey Meyers, "*For Whom the Bell Tolls* as Contemporary History," Council on Research and Creative Work, Distinguished Research Lecture Series no. 1 (Boulder, Colo.: University of Colorado, fall 1988): 1–19; hereafter cited in text.

2. Jeffrey Meyers, *Hemingway: A Biography* (New York: Harper and Row, 1985), 337.

3. Joseph Waldmeir, "Chapter Numbering and Meaning in *For Whom the Bell Tolls*," *The Hemingway Review* 8.2 (Spring 1989): 45.

4. John J. Teunissen, "*For Whom the Bell Tolls* as Mythic Narrative" in *Ernest Hemingway: Six Decades of Criticism*, ed. Linda W. Wagner (Ann

Arbor, Mich.: Michigan State University Press, 1987), 232. hereafter cited in text.

5. Edward F. Stanton, *Hemingway and Spain: A Pursuit* (Seattle and London: University of Washington Press, 1989), 166–72; hereafter cited in text.

6. D. E. Pohren, *Lives and Legends of Flamenco* (Madrid: Society of Spanish Studies, 1964), 148; hereafter cited in text.

7. Ernest Hemingway, *Nick Adams Stories* (New York: Charles Scribner's Sons, 1972), 238; hereafter cited in text as *NAS*.

8. Manuscript, University of Texas Library, p. 54. I am grateful to Robert W. Lewis for his transcription of the text.

9. *Diccionario enciclopédico ilustrado del flamenco*, eds. José Blas Vega and Manuel Ríos Ruiz (Madrid: Cinterco, 1988), vol. 1: 370–73.

10. Patrick Hemingway, interview, *USA Today*, 20 May 1986.

11. Cecil D. Eby, "The Real Robert Jordan" in *The Merrill Studies in* For Whom the Bell Tolls, ed. Sheldon Norman Grebstein (Columbus, Ohio: Merrill, 1971), 45.

10. The Action: Day One

1. Ernest Hemingway, ed., *Men at War* (New York: Bramhall House, 1979), xiv.

2. Earl Rovit, *Ernest Hemingway* (New York: Twayne, 1963), 136; hereafter cited in text.

3. My translation from Sandra Forman and Allen Josephs, *Only Mystery: Federico García Lorca's Poetry in Word and Image* (Gainesville, Fla.: University Press of Florida, 1992), 95; hereafter cited in text as Forman and Josephs.

11. The Action: Day Two

1. José Manuel Martínez Bande, *La ofensiva sobre Segovia y la batalla de Brunete* (Madrid: San Martín, 1972), 74–75.

2. Gerald Brenan, *South from Granada* (London: Penguin, 1963), 196; hereafter cited in text. There is an interesting reference to what may be Ronda in a letter from Joris Ivens to Hemingway (27 February 1940): "Fine that book is going ahead—like to read what the fascists did to us, because what we did to them is still vivid in my mind. That row of good people from bullring to the river." Cited in Norberto Fuentes, *Hemingway in Cuba* (Secaucus, N.J.: Lyle Stuart, 1984), 177; hereafter cited in text as Fuentes.

Notes and References

3. Robert E. Gajdusek, "Pilar's Tale: The Myth and the Message," *The Hemingway Review* 10.1 (Fall 1990): 25.

4. H. R. Stoneback, "'The Priest Did Not Answer': Hemingway, The Church, The Party and *For Whom the Bell Tolls*," in *Blowing the Bridge: Essays on Hemingway and* For Whom the Bell Tolls, ed. Rena Sanderson (New York: Greenwood, 1992), 107; hereafter cited in text.

5. Ernest Hemingway, *Green Hills of Africa* (New York: Scribner's, 1935), 72; hereafter cited in text as *GHA*; my emphasis.

6. Ernest Hemingway, *A Farewell to Arms* (New York: Scribner's, 1929), 116.

7. T. S. Eliot, *The Complete Poems and Plays 1909–1950* (New York: Harcourt, Brace and World, 1971), 117–22.

8. Michael Reynolds, *The Young Hemingway* (New York: Basil Blackwell, 1986), 208; hereafter cited in text.

9. Cited by Paul Smith, *A Reader's Guide to the Short Stories of Ernest Hemingway* (Boston: G. K. Hall, 1989), 255.

10. Elaine Pagels, *The Gnostic Gospels* (New York: Random House, 1979), 129.

11. See Margo Anand, *The Art of Sexual Ecstasy* (Los Angeles: Jeremy P. Tarcher, 1989), for a discussion of tantric sexuality. The phrase "the way in" comes from her study and the "Jacob's ladder" from a citation therein (42) from Elisabeth Haich's *Sexual Energy and Yoga*.

12. Gary Zukav, *The Dancing Wu Li Masters: An Overview of the New Physics* (New York: Bantam Books, 1980), 313; hereafter cited in text.

13. Cited in José María Blázquez, *Diccionario de las religiones prerromanas de Hispania* (Madrid: Ediciones Istmo, 1975), 74.

14. Carol Zaleski, *Otherworld Journeys: Accounts of Near-death Experience in Medieval and Modern Times* (New York: Oxford University Press, 1988), 12.

15. Colin Wilson, *Afterlife* (London: Harrap, 1985), 50.

12. The Action: Day Three

1. Allen Guttman, "Mechanized Doom: Ernest Hemingway and the Spanish Civil War," in *The Merrill Studies in* For Whom the Bell Tolls, ed. Sheldon Norman Grebstein, (Columbus, Ohio: Merrill, 1971), 78; Guttman's emphasis.

2. Kenneth S. Lynn, *Hemingway: The Life and The Work* (New York: Simon and Schuster, 1987), 474.

3. Gioia Diliberto, *Hadley* (New York: Ticknor and Fields, 1992), 79; hereafter cited in text.

13. The Action: Morning of the Fourth Day

1. Joel Hodson, "Robert Jordan Revisited: Hemingway's Debt to T. E. Lawrence," *The Hemingway Review* 10.2 (Spring 1992): 5.

2. William Braasch Watson, "Investigating Hemingway: The Story," *North Dakota Quarterly* 59.1 (Winter 1991): 39; hereafter cited in text as Watson, Winter 1991.

3. William Braasch Watson, "Investigating Hemingway: The Trip," *North Dakota Quarterly* 59.3 (Summer 1991): 91; hereafter cited in text as Watson, Summer 1991.

4. William Braasch Watson, "Investigating Hemingway: The Novel," *North Dakota Quarterly* 60.1 (Winter 1992): 1; hereafter cited in text as Watson 1992.

5. Robert E. Gajdusek, "Bridges: Their Creation and Destruction in the Works of Ernest Hemingway," in *Up in Michigan: Proceedings of the First National Conference of the Hemingway Society*, ed. Joseph J. Waldmeir (Traverse City, Mich.: Joseph J. Waldmeir, 1983), 80; hereafter cited in text as Gajdusek 1983.

6. "Roll, Jordan, Roll," transcribed and arranged by Hugo Frey, © 1924 (Renewed 1952) Robbins Music Co. The River Jordan is very strongly associated with "crossing over" to the Promised Land in spirituals such as "Deep River," "Swing Low, Sweet Chariot," "Every Time I Feel the Spring," and "Roll, Jordan, Roll." But only the latter makes a good football cheer (if the runner is named Jordan) as well. See also Hugo Frey, *Famous Negro Spirituals* (Miami, Fla.: Belwin, no date).

7. Warren Shibles, *Death: An Interdisciplinary Analysis* (Whitewater, Wis.: The Language Press, 1974), 368.

Appendix: On Language

1. Susan F. Beegel, *Hemingway's Craft of Omission* (Ann Arbor, Mich.: UMI Research Press, 1988), 57.

2. Martha Gellhorn, in conversation, Michigan State University Conference: International Literature of the Spanish Civil War, 21 November 1987.

3. Colin Wilson, *Eagle and Earwig* (London: John Baker, 1965), 124.

4. John J. Allen, "The English of Hemingway's Spaniards," *South Atlantic Bulletin* 27 (November 1961): 7.

5. Joseph Warren Beach, "Style in *For Whom the Bell Tolls*," *Ernest Hemingway: Critiques of Four Major Novels*, ed. Carlos Baker (New York: Scribner's, 1962), 84–86.

6. Betty Moore, *Ernest Hemingway and Spain: Growth of a "Spanish"*

Notes and References

Prose Style (Universidad de Valladolid: Publicaciones del Departamento de Inglés (9 September 1979): 232.

7. James R. Mellow, *Invented Lives: F. Scott and Zelda Fitzgerald* (Boston: Houghton Mifflin, 1984), 417.

Selected Bibliography

Primary Sources

Across the River and into the Trees. New York: Scribner, 1950.

By-line: Ernest Hemingway. Selected Articles and Dispatches of Four Decades. Edited by William White. New York: Scribner, 1967.

The Complete Short Stories of Ernest Hemingway. New York: Scribner, 1987.

The Dangerous Summer. Introduction by James Michener. New York: Scribner, 1985.

Death in the Afternoon. New York: Scribner, 1932.

88 Poems. Edited by Nicholas Gerogiannis. New York: Harcourt Brace Jovanovich, 1979.

Ernest Hemingway: Selected Letters, 1917–1961. Edited by Carlos Baker. New York: Scribner, 1981.

A Farewell to Arms. New York: Scribner, 1929.

The Fifth Column and Four Stories of the Spanish Civil War. New York: Scribner, 1972.

For Whom the Bell Tolls. New York: Scribner, 1940.

The Garden of Eden. New York: Scribner, 1986.

Green Hills of Africa. New York: Scribner, 1935.

Hemingway: The Wild Years. Edited and with an introduction by Gene Z. Hanrahan. New York: Dell Publishing, 1962.

in our time. Paris: Three Mountains Press, 1924.

In Our Time. New York: Boni and Liveright, 1925.

Islands in the Stream. New York: Scribner, 1970.

Men at War. Edited and with an introduction by Ernest Hemingway. New York: Crown Publishers, 1942.

Men without Women. New York: Scribner, 1927.

A Moveable Feast. New York: Scribner, 1964.

The Nick Adams Stories. Preface by Philip Young. New York: Scribner, 1972.

The Old Man and the Sea. New York: Scribner, 1952.

The Spanish Earth. Introduction by Jasper Wood. Cleveland, Ohio: J. B. Savage, 1938.

The Sun Also Rises. New York: Scribner, 1926.

To Have and Have Not. New York: Scribner, 1937.

The Torrents of Spring. New York: Scribner, 1926.

Winner Take Nothing. New York: Scribner, 1933.

Secondary Sources

Allen, John J. "The English of Hemingway's Spaniards" in *The Merrill Studies in* For Whom the Bell Tolls. Edited by Sheldon Norman Grebstein. Columbus, Ohio: Merrill, 1971. Analyzes the "Spanish" spoken in English.

Allen, Michael J. B. "The Unspanish War in *For Whom the Bell Tolls*." *Contemporary Literature* 13.2 (Spring 1972): 204–12. Sees Hemingway as mythmaker and novel as both realism and parable.

Baker, Carlos. *Ernest Hemingway: A Life Story*. New York: Charles Scribner's Sons, 1969. Still standard biography of Hemingway.

———. *The Writer as Artist*. Princeton, N.J.: Princeton University Press, 1972. Contains excellent essay on novel, "The Spanish Tragedy."

Barea, Arturo. "Not Spain but Hemingway," in *Studies in* For Whom the Bell Tolls. Edited by Sheldon Norman Grebstein. Columbus, Ohio: Merrill, 1971. Originally published in May 1941 *Horizon*; outlines all novel's faults from historical Spanish point of view.

Beach, Joseph Warren. "Style in *For Whom the Bell Tolls*" in *Ernest Hemingway: Critiques of Four Major Novels*. New York: Scribner's, 1962. High praise for Hemingway's "Spanish" in English and "Biblical" style.

Bessie, Alvah C. "A postscript," in *The Merrill Studies in* For Whom the Bell Tolls. Edited by Sheldon Norman Grebstein. Columbus, Ohio: Merrill, 1971. Update to Bessie's review.

Brasch, James D., and Joseph Sigman. *Hemingway's Library: A Composite*

Record. New York: Garland, 1981. Record of contents of library at Hemingway's house in Cuba.

Capellán, Angel. *Hemingway and the Hispanic World*. Ann Arbor, Mich.: UMI Research Press, 1985. Analysis of Hemingway's involvements in Spain.

Castillo-Puche, José Luis. *Hemingway in Spain*. Garden City, New York: Doubleday, 1974. Spanish novelist's recollections of Hemingway in Spain.

Cooper, Stephen. *The Politics of Ernest Hemingway*. Ann Arbor, Mich.: UMI Research Press, 1987. Analysis of Hemingway's politics.

Cortada, James W. *Historical Dictionary of the Spanish Civil War, 1936–1939*. Westport, Conn.: Greenwood, 1982. Reference guide to the Spanish Civil War.

Cowley, Malcolm. "A Portrait of Mr. Papa," *Life*, 10 January 1949. First important biographical sketch of Hemingway to appear.

Donaldson, Scott. *By Force of Will*. New York: Viking, 1977. Topical biography of Hemingway, good on communism.

Eby, Cecil D. "The Real Robert Jordan," in *The Merrill Studies in* For Whom the Bell Tolls. Edited by Sheldon Norman Grebstein. Columbus, Ohio: Merrill, 1971. Maintains Jordan was based on Major Robert Merriman of Lincoln Brigade.

Fenimore, Edward. "English and Spanish in *For Whom the Bell Tolls*" in *Ernest Hemingway: The Man and His Work*. Edited by John K. M. McCaffery. New York: Cooper Square, 1969. Analysis of language in novel, emphasizing primitive and fatalistic elements.

French, Warren. *The Social Novel at the End of an Era*. Carbondale, Ill.: Southern Illinois University Press, 1966. Examines political aspects of novel.

Fuentes, Norberto. *Hemingway in Cuba*. Secaucus, N.J.: Lyle Stuart, 1984. Contains numerous references to Hemingway's involvement in the Spanish Civil War.

Gajdusek, Robert E. "Bridges: Their Creation and Destruction in the Works of Ernest Hemingway," in *Up in Michigan: Proceedings of the First National Conference of the Hemingway Society*. Edited by Joseph J. Waldmeir. Traverse City, Mich.: Joseph J. Waldmeir, 1983. Interesting Jungian analysis of bridges, especially bridge in novel.

———. "Pilar's Tale: The Myth and the Message," *The Hemingway Review* 10.1 (Fall 1990): 19–33. Fine Jungian interpretation of Pilar's account of massacre.

———. "Is He Building a Bridge or Blowing One?: The Repossession of Text by the Author in *For Whom the Bell Tolls*." *The Hemingway Review* 11.2 (Spring 1992): 45–51. Continuation of first article with more metaphysical conclusion.

Gould, Thomas E. "'A Tiny Operation with Great Effect': Authorial Revision and Editorial Emasculation in the Manuscript of Hemingway's *For Whom the Bell Tolls*" in *Blowing the Bridge: Essays on Hemingway and* For Whom the Bell Tolls. Edited by Rena Sanderson. New York: Greenwood, 1992. Studies manuscript additions, especially sexual passages.

Guttman, Allen. "Mechanized Doom: Ernest Hemingway and the Spanish Civil War," in *The Merrill Studies in* For Whom the Bell Tolls. Edited by Sheldon Norman Grebstein. Columbus, Ohio: Merrill, 1971. Juxtaposes "primitive" culture of Spain and horror of modern warfare.

Hanneman, Audre. *Ernest Hemingway: A Comprehensive Bibliography*. Princeton, N.J.: Princeton University Press, 1967. First volume of comprehensive bibliography of Hemingway and his work.

————. *Supplement to Ernest Hemingway: A Comprehensive Bibliography*. Princeton, N. J.: Princeton University Press, 1975. Second volume, supplementing first and updating bibliography from 1966–1973.

Hemingway, Mary Welsh. *How It Was*. New York: Alfred A. Knopf, 1976. Hemingway's fourth wife's autobiography containing comments on locations.

Hodson, Joel. "Robert Jordan Revisited: Hemingway's Debt to T. E. Lawrence," *The Hemingway Review* 10.2 (Spring 1991): 2–16. Argues Jordan was based in part on T. E. Lawrence.

Hotchner, A. E. *Papa Hemingway*. New York: Random House, 1966. Biographical treatment of late period; claims to have seen cave that guerrillas used.

Josephs, Allen. "Hemingway's Poor Spanish: Chauvinism and Loss of Credibility in *For Whom the Bell Tolls*" in *Hemingway: A Revaluation*. Edited by Donald R. Noble. Troy, N.Y.: Whitston, 1983. Points out errors in Hemingway's Spanish.

Kert, Bernice. *The Hemingway Women*. New York: W. W. Norton & Co., 1983. Biographies of women, from their point of view, including material on Spanish Civil War.

Larson, Kelli A. *Ernest Hemingway: A Reference Guide, 1974–1989*. Boston: G. K. Hall, 1991. Third volume of bibliography.

Lewis, Robert W. *Hemingway on Love*. Austin, Tex.: University of Texas Press, 1965. Good analysis of love in Hemingway's fiction, with fine chapter on Robert and María.

de Madariaga, Salvador. "The World Weighs a Writer's Influence," *Saturday Review* 44, 29 July 1961. Elegy for Hemingway, concentrating on understanding of Spain.

Martínez Bande, José Manuel. *La ofensiva sobre Segovia y la batalla de*

Selected Bibliography

Brunete. Madrid: San Martín, 1972. Only book on real La Granja/Segovia Offensive.

Martin, Robert A. "Hemingway's *For Whom the Bell Tolls*: Fact into Fiction," *Studies in American Fiction* 15.2 (Spring 1987): 219–225. Sees novel as blend of real and invented.

Meyers, Jeffrey. *"For Whom the Bell Tolls* as Contemporary History," Council on Research and Creative Work: Distinguished Research Lecture Series. Boulder, Colo.: University of Colorado Graduate School, Fall 1988. Interesting historical interpretation of novel.

Meyers, Jeffrey, ed. *Hemingway: The Critical Heritage*. London: Routledge and Kegan Paul, 1982. Reprints reviews.

Moore, Betty. "Ernest Hemingway and Spain: The Growth of a 'Spanish' Prose Style." Universidad de Valladolid: Publicaciones del Departamento de Inglés (9 September 1979): 229–53. Studies "Spanish" in English.

Nakjavani, Erik. "Knowledge as Power: Robert Jordan as an Intellectual Hero." *Hemingway Review* 7.2 (Spring 1988): 131–46. Examines Jordan's rationality and ideas.

Rovit, Earl. *Ernest Hemingway*. New York: Twayne, 1963. Good general study of Hemingway's fiction.

Rudat, Wolfgang E. H. "Hemingway's Rabbit: Slips of the Tongue and Other Linguistic Games in *For Whom the Bell Tolls.*" *Hemingway Review* 10.1 (Fall 1990): 34–51. Maintains "rabbit" is English, not Spanish.

Sanderson, Rena, ed. *Blowing the Bridge: Essays on Hemingway and* For Whom the Bell Tolls. New York: Greenwood, 1992. Introduction has update of criticism of novel.

Stanton, Edward F. *Hemingway and Spain: A Pursuit*. Seattle and London: University of Washington Press, 1989. Full-length study of Hemingway and Spain.

Stephens, Robert O., ed. *Ernest Hemingway: The Critical Reception*. New York: Burt Franklins, 1977. Reprints reviews.

Stoneback, H. R. "'The Priest Did Not Answer': Hemingway, the Church, the Party" and *For Whom the Bell Tolls*, in *Blowing the Bridge: Essays on Hemingway and* For Whom the Bell Tolls. Edited by Rena Sanderson. New York: Greenwood, 1992. Fine analysis of meaning, political and spiritual, in novel.

Teunissen, John J. *"For Whom the Bell Tolls* as Mythic Narrative" in *Ernest Hemingway: Six Decades of Criticism*. Edited by Linda W. Wagner. Ann Arbor, Mich.: Michigan State University Press, 1987. Mythic interpretation of novel.

Thomas, Hugh. *The Spanish Civil War*. New York: Harper and Row, 1977. Extensive history of Spanish Civil War.

Van Gunten, Mark C. "The Polemics of Narrative and Difference in *For Whom the Bell Tolls*" in *Blowing the Bridge: Essays on Hemingway and For Whom the Bell Tolls*. Edited by Rena Sanderson. New York: Greenwood, 1992. Studies relation of reality and fiction in the novel.

Waldmeir, Joseph. "Chapter Numbering and Meaning in *For Whom the Bell Tolls*," *The Hemingway Review* 8.2 (Spring 1989): 43–45. Proposes Gertrude Stein as basis for character of Pilar.

Watson, William Braasch. "Hemingway's Spanish Civil War Dispatches," *The Hemingway Review* 7.2 (Spring 1988): 4–121. Publication with commentary of Hemingway's dispatches for North American Newspaper Alliance.

———. "Investigating Hemingway: The Story." *North Dakota Quarterly* 59.1 (Winter 1991): 38–68. Historian's view of behind-the-lines mission Hemingway may have participated in.

———. "Investigating Hemingway: The Trip." *North Dakota Quarterly* 59.3 (Summer 1991) 79–95. Reconstruction of alleged trip to Alfambra for behind-the-lines mission.

———. "Investigating Hemingway: The Novel." *North Dakota Quarterly* 60.1 (Winter 1992): 1–39. Studies what Hemingway knew about demolition.

———. "Joris Ivens and the Communists: Bringing Hemingway into the Spanish Civil War" in *Blowing the Bridge: Essays on Hemingway and For Whom the Bell Tolls*. Edited by Rena Sanderson. New York: Greenwood, 1992. Describes the history of the Dutch filmmaker's effort to indoctrinate Hemingway.

Williams, Wirt. *The Tragic Art of Ernest Hemingway*. Baton Rouge, La.: Louisana State University Press, 1981. Examines novel as tragedy.

Wyden, Peter. *The Passionate War: The Narrative History of the Spanish Civil War, 1936–1939*. New York: Simon and Schuster, 1983. Contains information about Hemingway during Spanish Civil War.

Index

Index

The Author

Allen Josephs is University Research Professor and Professor of Spanish in the Department of English and Foreign Languages at the University of West Florida, Pensacola, where he has taught since 1969. A founding member of the Hemingway Society, he has served on the Society's Executive Committee; serves on the Editorial Board of the *Hemingway Review*; and was On-site Director of the 5th International Hemingway Conference held in Pamplona, Spain, 15–21 July 1992. Author of *White Wall of Spain: The Mysteries of Andalusian Culture*, he has written many articles on Hemingway and Spain for publications such as the *Atlantic*, *Boston Review*, and *New York Times Book Review*, as well as publications in Spain and Latin America. His latest book (co-authored with Sandra Forman) is *Only Mystery: The Poetry of Federico García Lorca in Word and Image*. Currently he is at work on a new book about Spain and a book of essays on Hemingway.